W9-BUO-893

Praise for Par Fork!
THE GOLF RESORT COOKBOOK

"Gwen Ashley Walters is a genius at convincing exclusive resort chefs to part with their cooking secrets. In her latest book, she takes us into the kitchens of some of the finest golfing venues in the country for indulgent morning treats, light and lively lunches and downright grand slam dinners. You don't have to know a birdie from a bogie to appreciate that *Par Fork!* is packed with wonderful food, and you won't have to wear plaid pants to enjoy it."

— **Michael McLaughlin**,
food writer and cookbook author

"Forget the sweet spot, ignore your swing and head for the kitchen.
Gwen Ashley Walters' stories from dining rooms of leading and legendary American golf resorts had me planning several dinner parties. Still not sated, I'm calling my travel agent to plan a tour of these outstanding resorts, as Walters did in collecting the best recipes from Pinehurst to Pebble Beach."

— **Robin L. Kline**, MS, RD, CCP,
Savvy Food Communications

"A hole-in-one! Gwen Ashley Walters captures the excitement of top golf courses merged with recipes for memorable, delicious meals. This is truly a multi-course delight, in all ways."

— **Antonia Allegra**,
author, editor, and Director of the
Symposium for Professional Food Writers at The Greenbrier

Praise for Gwen Ashley Walters' other books:

"[*The Cool Mountain Cookbook*] continues to be one of my all-time favorites. The recipes are blessedly user-friendly, and the dishes never fail to impress."

— **Kyle Wagner**,
Denver Post restaurant critic

"Walters' [*The Great Ranch Cookbook*] is an original, mouthwatering collection that wins as both travel guide and dinner bell."
— *Today's Librarian*

"Walters' brings together hearty, warming recipes from America's top ski lodges."
— *ALA Booklist*

"Walters' cookbooks are easy to read as well as fun and informative."
— **Lynn Cline**,
The Santa Fe New Mexican

Par Fork!

THE GOLF RESORT COOKBOOK

Enjoy

Ashley Waller

Par Fork!

THE GOLF RESORT COOKBOOK

Gwen Ashley Walters, CCP

Illustrations by Betsy B. Hillis

Pen & Fork
COMMUNICATIONS

Par Fork! The Golf Resort Cookbook

Copyright ©2003 by Gwen Ashley Walters

All rights reserved. No part of this book may be reproduced or utilized in any form or by any means, electronic or mechanical, including photocopying, recording, or by any information storage or retrieval system, without permission in writing from the Publisher. Inquiries should be addressed to the Publisher.

Published by

P.O. Box 5165
Carefree, AZ 85377

www.penandfork.com

Front cover photo: Pinehurst Golf Resort, Pinehurst, NC
Photo by Michael Romney

Back cover photos (L to R):
Jeffrey S. Walters (food shots)
The Lodge at Pebble Beach (Links #9). Reprinted by permission of Pebble Beach Company.

Edited by Olin B. Ashley

Cover by Christy Moeller-Mosel, ATG Productions, Inc., Avondale, Arizona

Interior design by Michele DeFilippo, 1106 Design, llc Phoenix, Arizona

Printed in Hong Kong
First Edition

Publisher's Cataloging-in-Publication Data

Walters, Gwen Ashley.
   Par fork! : the golf resort cookbook / Gwen Ashley
Walters. -- 1st ed.
   p. cm.
   Includes index.
   LCCN 2002190445
   ISBN 0-9663486-2-1

   1. Cookery. 2. Menus. 3. Golf resorts–United
States–Guidebooks. I. Title.

TX714.W2628 2003   641.5

Dedication

For Jeff, always

Also by Gwen Ashley Walters, CCP

The Great Ranch Cookbook:
Spirited Recipes and Rhetoric from America's Best Ranches

The Cool Mountain Cookbook:
A Gourmet Guide to Winter Retreats

www.penandfork.com

Photo Credits:

All food photography by Jeffrey S. Walters unless otherwise noted.

Page:	Source:
P-1	Property photo reprinted by permission of Pebble Beach Company.
P-2	Property photo courtesy of The Broodmoor.
P-3	Property photo courtesy of The Lodge at Koele.
P-4	Property and food photos courtesy of Manele Bay Hotel.
P-5	Property photo reprinted by permission of Bandon Dunes, Wood Sabold Photography.
P-6	Property photo courtesy of The Boulders Resort.
P-7	Property photo courtesy of The Fairmont Scottsdale Princess Resort.
P-8	Property photo courtesy of The Lodge at Ventana Canyon.
P-9	Property photo courtesy of Loews Ventana Canyon.
P-10	Property photo courtesy of The Phoenician.
P-11	Property photo courtesy of Barton Creek Resort.
P-12	Property photo courtesy of the Hyatt Regency Coconut Point.
P-13	Property photo courtesy of Doral Golf Resort & Spa.
P-14	Property photo courtesy of the Hyatt Regency Grand Cypress.
P-15	Property photo courtesy of The Cloister at Sea Island.
P-16	Property photo courtesy of Pinehurst Resort, photo by Michael Romney.
P-17	Property photo courtesy of The Homestead Resort.
P-18	Property photo courtesy of The Greenbrier.
P-19	Property photo courtesy of The Sagamore.
P-20	Golf course photos courtesy of The Lodge at Pebble Beach, photo by Rob Brown (top); The Broadmoor (middle); The Lodge at Koele (bottom).
P-21	Golf course photos courtesy of The Cloister at Sea Island (top left); Manele Bay Hotel (top right); The Phoenician (lower right).
P-22	Golf course photos courtesy of the Hyatt Regency Grand Cypress (top); The Boulders Resort (middle); Pinehurst Resort (bottom).
P-23	Golf course photos courtesy of The Greenbrier (top); The Lodge at Ventana Canyon (middle); Doral Golf Resort & Spa (bottom).
P-24	Golf course photos courtesy of The Sagamore (middle); The Homestead Resort, photo by Donnelle Oxley (bottom).

Table of Contents

Content by Resort

THE WEST

THE SOUTHWEST

THE SOUTHEAST

THE NORTHEAST

Content by Recipe

Introduction

They say that golf is so-named because certain other well-known four-letter words were already taken. Golf can be a frustrating game, right? But we still go back out there, don't we? Why? Because golf is a challenge. One perfect shot, ringing true on the sweet spot, is all it takes to remind us why we spend countless hours in the pursuit of a little white ball. Golf is an unmatched escape, a respite from the rigors of routine. It's a prized chance to be outdoors, inhaling fresh air while enjoying the company of fellow golfers, and sharpening our swings and strokes. There is no greater game.

Golfers share many common traits, including a love of fine food, as evidenced by the award-winning cuisine served in the top golf resorts around the country. If golfers weren't fussy when it comes to food, these resorts would not spend the resources they do to employ the best chefs and provide them with state-of-the-art kitchens in which to work their magic. Thankfully, we don't have to settle for burgers and hotdogs after a grueling day on the links. We're treated to prime aged beef, fresh-from-the-ocean fish, free-range chickens, and countless other tantalizing meals, all expertly prepared and served in style.

This book is special because I get to share with you the finest golf resorts across the country. Three of them are personally special to me. I learned how to play golf at Pinehurst in the summer of 1993, and I completed my culinary externship at the renowned Boulders resort in 1997. I spent time honing my writing skills at the beautiful Greenbrier Resort, where I had the pleasure of meeting and lunching with Julia Child. And the others? Well, I've just enjoyed visiting them, playing golf, and eating exquisite food. The number of awards bestowed upon these resorts is astounding, and combined, would fill an entire book. These are the best of the best.

This book is a celebration of these peerless resorts, their golf, and their food. The travel vignettes explore each resort's uniqueness and its contribution to the game of golf. The recipes embrace the spirit of the resorts, the essence of superb food prepared by great chefs with the freshest ingredients. So turn the page and travel with me to our country's most-loved golf resorts. Afterwards, head into the kitchen to recreate some of the delicious fare these resorts so kindly shared with me. Let the celebration begin!

Travel Tips

J've done my best to accurately present the facts as well as the personal descriptions of each resort. I hope you enjoy this book and that it will help you find a place that fits your idea of a dream golf vacation. But before you make your plans, I suggest that you read the following points to help you make your decision.

- All rates listed in this book represent the 2003 season. Unless otherwise noted, the rate represents 1 night's lodging only, per person based on double occupancy. Those resorts that offer the Modified American Plan (including breakfast and dinner in the lodging rate) are so noted. Golf is not included in any lodging rate.

$	less than $200
$$	$201–300
$$$	$301–400
$$$$	$401 and higher

- Call the resort to verify the rate and ask if there are other packages you might consider. Most of the resorts have different pricing for different times of the year. Many offer lower rates in what they call their "shoulder" seasons, typically in the spring and fall.
- Ask about golf packages. Most resorts bundle tee times and often other related services as part of a one-price deal.
- Ask about dress code for the golf course and all the dining options on property.
- Ask about arrival and departure times and transportation options.

These tips are only suggestions. I'm sure you will think of other questions to ask as you plan your vacation. The most important thing is to select a destination that offers the activities, food, and ambiance you expect. All of the resorts in this book are destinations worth visiting. Some will appeal to more of your interests than others will. My hope is that through this book, you will find golf destinations that exceed your expectations. Let me know what your experience is, from making a reservation to spending time at the resort, including the things you like and don't like.

To e-mail me, visit my website at: ***http://www.penandfork.com***

Recipe for Success

Every single recipe in this book was tested and re-tested in my home kitchen in Scottsdale. My neighbor, Marilyn Robertson, re-tested a number of recipes for me. I know these recipes will work for you in your kitchen. I changed the recipes only when necessary to make them easier, without compromising the integrity of the dish. You will find a good mix of easy and challenging recipes.

If you run into any problems or have any questions about the recipes, ingredients, or procedures, contact me through my website (***www.penandfork.com***) and I will help you. Read through the points I've outlined below to help ensure your success. But if that doesn't help, I'm only a digital link away.

- The most important advice I can give you is to read the recipe all the way through before you start, even before you go to the grocery store to buy the ingredients. The directions might tell you to start a process the night before.
- *Mise en Place.* This is the French term for "everything in its place." It means gathering all the ingredients and equipment (and reading the entire recipe) before you begin. This will save you precious time and more than likely determine your success more than any other tip I could give you.
- I've listed times for certain recipe steps, like reducing wine or other liquids, or cooking until the mixture is thickened, etc. The directions might say, "reduce the liquid until only ¼ cup remains, about 15 minutes." These times are how long it took me to get the reduction to the right amount of residual liquid, using my pans. It might take you more or less time because you might use a different pan than I did. The width of the pan and the amount of heat can dramatically impact how long it takes to reduce something. In general, the wider the pan and the higher the heat, the quicker the reduction.
- Watch for the word "divided" in the ingredient list. It means that ingredient will be used more than once in the recipe. The directions will tell you how to divide the ingredient.
- Measure ingredients in the appropriate utensils. Use metal measuring cups for dry ingredients, such as flour, sugar, chopped carrots, etc. Level off with a straight edge across the top of the cup for the appropriate measurement. Use glass or plastic measuring cups with spouts for liquid ingredients such as water, milk, honey, etc. Get down to eye level for more accurate measuring, or use one of those cups designed to be read from the top. I have to thank my neighbor, Malen, for giving me one such cup made by OXO.
- Set cooking and baking times for 5 to 10 minutes less than the shortest time given in a recipe. Different ovens cook at different temperatures, and I don't want you to overcook something because your oven cooks hotter than mine does.

Across all recipes:
- Brown sugar is light brown sugar and packed tight.
- Butter is unsalted.
- Eggs are large, about 2 ounces each.
- Flour is all-purpose.
- Milk is whole milk, unless otherwise noted.
- Onions can be either white or yellow if not specified. I tend to buy yellow onions more than white, and experts say yellow ones are a bit stronger tasting.
- Preferred vegetable oil is canola, though sunflower and corn oils are acceptable.
- Spinach, lettuces, and herbs are soaked in cold water to remove dirt then dried before using.
- Salt is kosher salt; if you use regular table salt, reduce the quantity by about one quarter. Using regular salt will make the dishes taste too salty if you don't reduce the quantity.

Common Procedures

Demi-glace

Many recipes call for "demi-glace" which, in the traditional French sense, is a highly-reduced, gelatinous sauce of half brown sauce, half veal stock. I use a brand of demi-glace called Custom Master's Touch Sauce Bases. It's easy to prepare; combining 3 tablespoons of the demi-glace per 1 cup of boiling water. I find it in the refrigerated section at A. J.'s Fine Foods (the Pima Road location). You can order it from A. J.'s if your store doesn't carry it. See Sources, page 203.

There are other products, however, including Williams-Sonoma's "Forgotten Tradition" and More Than Gourmet's "Demi-Glace." See Sources, page 203, for ordering information. Another option is the use of homemade beef stock or reduced sodium beef broth or reconstituted beef bouillon, although this option requires either a roux or a slurry to thicken the mixture.

A **roux** is equal parts (by weight) of fat and flour (for example, ½ an ounce of butter (1 tablespoon) and ½ an ounce of flour (2 tablespoons) which is cooked for a few minutes until it turns golden. Then the cooked roux is mixed into the hot broth and simmered until it thickens and the starch taste disappears, about 15 minutes. Use the ratio of 1 tablespoon of butter and 2 tablespoons of flour per cup of broth. Once thickened, this sauce may be substituted for the demi-glace as you proceed with the recipe.

A **slurry** is a mixture of equal parts cold water and cornstarch or arrowroot. The boiling broth will thicken immediately when the slurry is added. Remember that it will thicken only if the liquid is boiling. Use 1 tablespoon of cold water and 1 tablespoon of cornstarch per cup of broth.

Both options produce a slightly salty sauce, so do not add any more salt without first tasting. Either method will produce a substitute for demi-glace, though neither will have the depth of flavor of a demi-glace.

continued on next page

Roasting Garlic

Heat oven to 350°F. Cut top third off, exposing cloves. Brush with olive oil, wrap in foil, and place in a roasting pan. Roast in the oven for 45 to 60 minutes, or until cloves are golden brown. Cool and remove cloves from papery shell. Will keep, covered, in the refrigerator for 2 weeks.

Roasting Peppers

The preferred method is over an open flame. Puncture the peppers once or twice with the tip of a knife to allow steam to escape while roasting. Hold the pepper just inches from an open flame until the skin blackens, turning the pepper to blacken all the skin. The better job of blackening the skin, the easier the pepper will be to peel. I bought a chile pepper grate from the Santa Fe School of Cooking (see Sources, page 205) that I place on my gas-stove burner in the kitchen. I can roast several peppers at a time this way, without having to stand there the whole time, holding the pepper with tongs. I have noticed that the metal grate gets so hot that it warps a little, but if I let it cool at room temperature afterwards, it seems to return to its normal flat shape.

After the peppers are black all over, I place them in a large stainless steel bowl, cover them with plastic wrap, and let them steam until cool enough to handle. Then I peel the skin off, using a knife to scrape any stubborn parts. I DO NOT rinse the peppers under water. I think that washes away most of the flavor. I know some chefs do, but why bother roasting to get that charred flavor only to wash it down the drain?

Another option, though not as flavorful, is to heat oven to 350° to 375°F. Lightly oil peppers and make a tiny slit in the top or bottom to allow steam to escape. Place on a baking sheet and bake for 30 to 50 minutes, turning often. Skin will blister and look like it is separating from the flesh and may even turn brown/black. Follow the directions above to steam, cool, and peel.

Toasting Hazelnuts

Heat oven to 350°F. Spread hazelnuts on a sheet pan and roast for 15 to 18 minutes, just until the skins darken and start to crack. Careful or they will burn, but you need to give them as much time as you can to bring out the flavor. Remove from the oven and cool. You will hear a lot of crackling as they cool. Once cooled, place a handful or two in a kitchen towel and rub vigorously. Most of the skins will come off, but don't worry if some don't. Repeat the process until all the nuts have been skinned.

Toasting Other Nuts

Heat oven to 350°F. Spread nuts on a sheet pan and bake for 5 to 7 minutes or until fragrant, stirring occasionally. The exception is sliced almonds. Sometimes they take less than 5 minutes to toast. Set the timer for 3 minutes and then add more time if necessary.

Toasting Coconut

Heat oven to 350° F. Spread coconut on an ungreased sheet pan and bake for 7 to 10 minutes, or until golden brown, stirring often. A fork works best for fluffing and stirring.

The West

The Lodge
PEBBLE BEACH

17-Mile Drive
Pebble Beach, CA 93953
800.654.9300
www.pebblebeach.com

Golf Courses:
Pebble Beach Golf Links/
Spyglass Hill/Links at
Spanish Bay/Del Monte

Designers:
Jack Neville & Douglas
Grant/Robert T. Jones, Sr./
Jones, Jr., Tom Watson
& Frank Tatum/
Charles Maud

Available holes: 72

Accommodations:
161 guestrooms,
including suites

Rates: $$$$

Other Activities:
Spa, Beach & Tennis Club,
Equestrian Center,
shopping

Using simple word association, mention "famous golf resort," and the first likely answer is The Lodge at Pebble Beach. Even non-golfers understand the powerful lure of this legend-in-its-own-time golf sovereignty. Almost as famous as the Pebble Beach Golf Links are three more courses under the Pebble Beach umbrella. The Scottish-style Links at Spanish Bay and Spyglass Hill offer dramatic seaside holes, while the inland Del Monte course opened in 1897 still challenges golfers after more than a century of play.

Mass awareness of the Pebble Beach golfing monarchy resulted from the celebrity status of the star-studded Crosby Pro-Am, first played at the resort in 1947. Renamed the AT&T National Pebble Beach Pro-Am, what began as Bing Crosby's old "clambake" is now one of the most popular stops on the PGA tour.

The Californian-inspired architecture of the main lodge, a strikingly understated white edifice with clean lines, is embellished simply but elegantly with plantation shutters, coifed topiaries, and brass door handles. The rooms on the upper floor of The Lodge and in the 11 surrounding buildings are particularly spacious at an average of 650 square feet, and tastefully decorated with traditional and contemporary furnishings.

Dining is just as quietly elegant as the surroundings. Club XIX's formal setting is stylishly updated with contemporary French cuisine. Stillwater Bar & Grill specializes in the finest fresh seafood, including the Monterey Bay red abalone, a large mollusk native to northern California. The Tap Room, a favorite with golfers, is patterned after a proper English pub and serves traditional American fare plus a long list of handcrafted beers. And if these options aren't enough, the Inn at Spanish Bay is home to an Italian restaurant as well as the Asian fusion restaurant Roy's. Golfing at Pebble Beach is a dream come true for most golfers. The resort makes sure the dream continues through dinner.

Breakfast Menu

- GRANOLA WITH MONTMORENCY DRIED CHERRIES

- WHITE PLATE EGG SPECIAL

- CASA HEALTH BARS

Dinner Menu

- CRAB CAKES WITH CITRUS AÏOLI

- FENNEL & ENDIVE SLAW WITH CITRUS VINAIGRETTE

- RED WINE-BRAISED BEEF SHORT RIBS

- STRAWBERRY & RHUBARB CRISP

- *Recipe included*

Golf Pro's Tip

Cut out the fat. The word "fat" is a negative word shared by both culinary experts and golfers. If you're hitting the ball fat, try moving the ball back in your stance, or if you're headed to the driving range try this: place a tee in the ground about 2 inches in front of the ball. Work on hitting the tee and clipping it out of the ground when the ball happens to get in the way. If that doesn't work, there's always tennis.

Signature Hole

Pebble Beach course, Number 7 — scenic par 3 marches straight to the ocean, with the wind a factor all 106 yards to the green and an unruly gallery of crashing waves.

Granola with Montmorency Dried Cherries

You can feed a small army with this recipe. It freezes well, and it also makes a great gift. Dried sour cherries have a wonderful sweet tart taste that pleasantly sets off the juices in the back of your mouth. Sesame seeds and almonds are savory complements to the bright cherry taste.

MAKES 21 CUPS

1 (15-ounce) jar of wheat germ
1 (18-ounce) container
   old-fashioned oats
1½ cups coconut
1 cup (4¾ ounces) sesame seeds
1 cup (4¼ ounces) hulled
   sunflower seeds
1 cup slivered almonds

⅓ cup vegetable oil
1¼ cups honey
1 teaspoon vanilla extract
1 cup brown sugar
1 cup sugar
2 cups (10 ounces) dried sour
   or tart cherries

1. Heat oven to 300°F. Toss first 6 ingredients (wheat germ through almonds) together in a large bowl.

2. Heat next 5 ingredients (oil through sugars) in a saucepan over medium heat. Stir until sugars dissolve, but don't boil. Turn heat to low if mixture starts to boil and sugars aren't quite dissolved.

3. Pour warm oil mixture over oat mixture. Spread evenly on 2 lightly greased baking sheets (with sides) and bake until golden brown, about 20 to 25 minutes, stirring every 7 to 10 minutes to promote even browning. (Rotate pans often if baking at the same time on separate racks, or bake 1 pan at a time.)

4. Remove from oven and stir in dried cherries. Stir occasionally while cooling to break up lumps. Store at room temperature in an airtight container for up to 1 month, or up to 3 months in the freezer.

White Plate Special

There is nothing diner-style about this white plate special that begins with a chile-spiked egg white base, topped with steamed spinach, and finally capped with an earthy, herb-roasted portabella mushroom. The roasted red pepper sauce completes the dish. It tastes as good as it looks. (See photograph on page P-1.)

SERVES 4

4 small portabella mushrooms
   (about 12 ounces total)
4 sprigs rosemary
4 stems basil (with leaves)
¼ cup vegetable stock (divided)
10 egg whites
1 teaspoon water
Pinch red pepper flakes

Salt and freshly ground white pepper
1 teaspoon olive oil
4 cups (2 ounces) spinach, washed,
   stemmed, and dried
1 teaspoon balsamic vinegar
1 cup chopped roasted red bell
   pepper*

1. Heat oven to 350°F. Remove mushroom stems and clean caps with a paper towel. Place the mushrooms gill-side down in a small roasting pan. Stuff a sprig of rosemary and a basil stem underneath each cap. Sprinkle mushrooms with 2 tablespoons of vegetable stock. Cover with foil. Roast for 15 minutes or until tender. When roasted, remove from oven, reserving mushroom juices. Slice mushroom caps at an angle into ¼-inch slices. Keep warm. While mushrooms are roasting, prepare the eggs, spinach, and roasted red bell pepper sauce.

2. Whisk egg whites with water, chili flakes, ¼ teaspoon of salt, and a pinch of white pepper. Spray an ovenproof nonstick skillet with nonstick spray. Heat over medium heat. When warm, pour in beaten egg whites. Gently run a spatula around the edges while the eggs are cooking, but don't stir. When the eggs' edges start to set, about 2 to 3 minutes, place skillet in 350°F oven to finish cooking. Remove from oven when eggs are completely set, about 5 minutes. Gently slide eggs onto a cutting board. Cut 4 circles with a 3 to 3½-inch cookie cutter. Keep warm.

3. Heat oil in a skillet over medium heat. Stir in spinach, balsamic vinegar, and a pinch of salt. Cover and cook over medium heat until spinach is wilted and tender, about 2 minutes.

4. Heat roasted red bell pepper with remaining 2 tablespoons of vegetable stock in a small saucepan over medium heat. When hot, remove from heat and purée in a blender. (CAUTION: hot liquids shoot straight up in a blender, so cover the top with a towel and hold lid down with pressure before turning machine on.) Season with salt and white pepper. May be made 2 days in advance. Store covered in the refrigerator, and gently reheat before serving.

5. Putting it all together: place an egg white round on a warm plate. Top with a spoonful of spinach and then a few sliced mushrooms. Drizzle plate with reserved mushroom juices and dot plate with roasted red bell pepper sauce.

Buy roasted red bell peppers in a jar, or see page 18 under Common Procedures for how to roast peppers.

Casa Health Bars

Not all my tasters liked this health bar recipe. In fact, I went and picked up remaining bars that some of my ungrateful tasters shunned, and I've since eaten them all myself. It's a health bar, people — not a cookie! I love the spicy ginger taste and the hint of licorice from the anise seeds. Trust me, these wouldn't be in the book if I didn't think you'd like them, too. I've since made another batch and keep them in the freezer for that next hike.

MAKES 16 BARS

1½ cups cake flour
¾ cup whole wheat flour
⅔ cup sesame seeds
⅔ cup brown sugar
½ cup wheat germ
½ cup old-fashioned oats
2 tablespoons orange zest
1 tablespoon anise seed
4 teaspoons hulled sunflower seeds
1 teaspoon baking powder
1 teaspoon baking soda

¾ teaspoon salt
3 eggs
½ cup applesauce
5 tablespoons vegetable oil
1½ teaspoons vanilla extract
1¼ cups (8 ounces) chopped dates
¾ cup (4 ounces) dried blueberries
2 tablespoons (½ ounce) finely
    chopped crystallized ginger
½ cup (2 ounces) dried tart cherries

1. Heat the oven to 350°F. Mix first 12 ingredients (cake flour through salt) together. (The resort suggests using a dough hook attachment on a stand mixer, but you can mix this by hand.)

2. Mix in the next 4 ingredients (eggs through vanilla) until combined. Fold in the remaining 4 ingredients (dates through dried cherries).

3. Divide dough in half and form each into a log 12 inches long, 3½ inches wide and 1-inch high. Place dough on sheet pans and score 1½-inch strips down the bar to create 8 bars per log. To score, cut all the way through the log, but don't separate the bars.

4. Bake for 12 to 15 minutes, until golden brown. Cut through the score marks and separate the bars. Place on a rack to cool completely. Keeps 4 days at room temperature in an airtight container, or up to 3 months frozen. To freeze, tightly wrap each bar individually in plastic wrap then store in a freezer bag.

Crab Cakes

WITH CITRUS AÏOLI

I'm a huge crab cake fan, but I'm often disappointed when I order them at a restaurant because I can't seem to find the crab among all the filler. Fortunately, these are heavy on the crab and light on the filler. Avoid regular grocery store canned crab. I've found really plump, sweet crabmeat at my specialty grocery store, A. J.'s Fine Foods. I've also discovered a good brand of imported lump crabmeat called Phillips, at Costco, a price warehouse club. Panko are Japanese bread crumbs, much lighter and crunchier than American crumbs. You'll find them in the Asian food section at most grocery stores. (See photograph on page P-1.)

MAKES 7 (3-INCH) CAKES

1 pound cooked lump crab meat
1 teaspoon olive oil
½ cup finely chopped celery
⅓ cup finely chopped fennel bulb
¼ cup mayonnaise
1 tablespoon chopped tarragon
1 tablespoon chopped parsley
2 teaspoons lemon zest

Salt and freshly ground black pepper
1 egg
½ cup flour
2 eggs, beaten
1½ cups panko (Japanese
   bread crumbs)
Vegetable oil for frying

1. Pick over crab to remove any shells. Blot with paper towels if excessively moist.

2. Heat olive oil in a small skillet over medium heat. When hot, add celery and fennel. Cook until vegetables are tender, about 2 to 3 minutes. Remove from heat to cool.

3. Mix crabmeat, cooled vegetables, mayonnaise, herbs, and lemon zest together until well combined. Taste and season with salt and pepper. Beat in 1 egg until well combined. Cover and chill in the refrigerator for at least 1 hour, up to 4 hours.

4. Set up a breading station with the flour in 1 bowl, the 2 beaten eggs in another bowl, and the panko in a third bowl.

5. Heat a large skillet over medium heat. Pour in enough oil to come to a ¼-inch depth. While the pan is heating, prepare the crab cakes.

6. Scoop 3-ounce portions, roughly ⅓ cup. (A #12 ice cream scoop is ⅓ cup.) Form into patties, about 3 inches in diameter.

7. First dip in flour to lightly coat cake, dusting off excess. Dip in beaten egg then roll in panko to completely cover. Heat the oven to 350°F. You can prepare the cakes up to this point and store covered in the refrigerator, up to 4 hours.

8. Fry cakes until golden brown on both sides, about 3 minutes per side. Place on a baking sheet and finish cooking in the oven until done, about 5 to 8 minutes. Serve with Citrus Aïoli.

Citrus Aïoli (Makes 1 cup)
1 cup mayonnaise
Zest of 1 lemon
1 teaspoon lemon juice
Zest of 1 lime
1 teaspoon lime juice
Salt and freshly ground white pepper

Mix first 5 ingredients (mayonnaise through lime juice) together. Season with salt and white pepper to taste. May be prepared 2 days in advance. Store covered in the refrigerator.

Fennel & Endive Slaw

WITH CITRUS VINAIGRETTE

*T*he Lodge serves this crisp, tart slaw underneath the crunchy crab cakes (see previous recipe). You can make the citrus vinaigrette ahead of time, but wait to slice the fennel and endive until you're ready to serve to keep the salad fresh and bright. For super thin fennel, use a mandoline or slicer. Try to find purple-tinged Belgian endive to add a color contrast to the pale fennel.

SERVES 4

Vinaigrette:
¼ cup grapefruit juice
2 tablespoons orange juice
1 tablespoon lemon juice
1 tablespoon champagne or
    white wine vinegar
1 teaspoon chopped fresh tarragon
½ teaspoon minced shallots
¼ teaspoon minced garlic

¼ cup extra virgin olive oil
Salt and freshly ground white pepper

Slaw:
1 fennel bulb thinly shaved
    (about 2 cups)
2 to 3 small Belgian endive (5 ounces)
    thinly sliced lengthwise
1 tablespoon chopped parsley
2 teaspoons chopped tarragon

1. Whisk (or blend in blender) the first 7 ingredients (grapefruit juice through garlic) together. Slowly whisk in olive oil (or drizzle into blender with machine on).

2. Season with salt and pepper to taste. May be made 3 days in advance. Store covered in the refrigerator, up to 3 days.

3. Toss fennel with endive and herbs. Drizzle with 2 to 3 tablespoons of vinaigrette and toss again.

Red Wine-Braised Beef Short Ribs

*H*ere's how to make an inexpensive cut of meat taste like a million bucks. The flavor takes me back to memories of my mom's Sunday pot roast. That's likely because these 3-inch ribs are cut from the chuck, just under the shoulder of the steer, the usual pot roast cut. Roasted potatoes or even mashed potatoes with fresh herbs would be great with these fall-off-the-bone tender ribs.

SERVES 4

2 tablespoons olive oil
5 pounds beef short ribs
Salt and freshly ground black pepper
½ cup flour
2 cups chopped onion
1 cup chopped celery
1 cup peeled and chopped carrot
1 cup peeled and chopped turnip

2 Roma tomatoes, seeded and
  chopped
1 tablepoon minced garlic
1 tablepoon tomato paste
4 sprigs fresh thyme
4 sprigs fresh oregano
½ teaspoon black peppercorns
4 cups red wine (such as burgundy)
4 cups beef stock, hot

1. Heat oven to 300°F. Heat olive oil in a roasting pan over medium-high heat. Rub ribs with salt and pepper, then dust with flour. When pan is very hot, and working in batches to avoid overcrowding, sear ribs on all sides until brown. Remove and cover with foil to keep warm.

2. Add next 6 ingredients (onion through garlic) to the pan and cook until onions begin to soften, about 3 minutes, stirring frequently. Stir in tomato paste. Cook until tomato paste darkens a bit, about 3 to 4 minutes. Stir in herbs and peppercorns.

3. Place the ribs meaty side down on top of the vegetables in a single layer. Pour the wine over the ribs. Turn the heat to high and bring to a boil. Reduce heat to a strong simmer, letting the wine reduce for about 5 minutes. Pour in the beef stock. Cover and bake until ribs are tender, about 2½ to 3 hours.

4. Remove ribs and strain sauce, discarding solids. Season with salt and pepper. Pour sauce over ribs.

Strawberry Rhubarb Crisp
WITH HONEY WHIPPED CREAM

$\mathcal{B}$aked in individual custard cups or ramekins, these are so adorable. The buttery, crunchy top covers a thick, sweet tart filling. Although I think it's best warm, I did sample one at room temperature and still licked the cup clean. The honey whipped cream helps mellow the tartness of the filling. A scoop of vanilla ice cream would do the trick, too. You can bake these 1 day in advance. Just cool and store covered in the refrigerator. To reheat, place uncovered in a preheated 300°F oven until heated completely through, about 15 minutes.

SERVES 8

Filling:
1½ pounds fresh rhubarb, sliced
　½-inch thick (about 5 cups)
¾ pound fresh strawberries, hulled
　and quartered (about 3 cups)
½ cup sugar
½ cup brown sugar
2 tablespoons instant tapioca
　mix (dry)
Pinch of nutmeg

Crisp topping:
8 tablespoons (1 stick) butter,
　slightly softened
½ cup plus 2 tablespoons sugar
½ cup plus 2 tablespoons
　brown sugar
1¼ cups flour

Honey Whipped Cream:
1 cup heavy whipping cream
2 tablespoons honey
Powdered sugar for dusting
Fresh mint (optional)

1. Stir filling ingredients together (rhubarb through nutmeg) and let stand for 20 minutes.

2. Heat oven to 350°F. Toss topping ingredients together with a fork or work with your hands until mixture looks like pea-size crumbles.

3. Spray 8 (8-ounce) custard cups with nonstick spray. Divide filling equally between the cups. Generously cover with the crisp topping (about ¼ cup per custard cup), mounding slightly. The filling and topping will shrink after baking.

4. Place cups on a baking sheet and bake until topping is golden brown and filling is bubbly, about 25 to 30 minutes. Cool for 10 to 15 minutes before serving.

5. Whip heavy cream until soft peaks form, about 2 minutes with an electric mixer on high speed. Drizzle in honey and continue whipping until stiff. To serve, place a custard cup on a plate. Dust with powdered sugar and place a dollop of Honey Whipped Cream on top. Garnish with fresh mint.

CRISPS, CRUNCHES, CRUMBLES AND COBBLERS

With so many names, sorting the categories can be challenging. Is a crisp the same thing as a crunch? Where do cobblers fit in? To add to the confusion, throw in a pandowdy, a buckle, and a brown betty. One thing is certain; all of them start with fruit. After that, things get a little less clear. Another component is either a crumb topping or a batter, and the batter can be biscuit-like or cake-like. Here are some definitions to de-mystify the terminology.

Crumb topping — a mixture of grains (such as flour, oats, or bread crumbs), butter, sugar, spices, and sometimes nuts. Many crumb toppings are called streusel toppings. Streusel is the German word for "sprinkle" or "strew", which is how crumb toppings are generally applied to cakes, muffins, crisps, and the others.

Crisp — sweetened fruit with thickened juices, topped with a crumb mixture and baked (like the Strawberry & Rhubarb Crisp on the preceding page). Crisps may be baked in individual serving dishes or in one larger baking dish.

Crunch — sweetened fruit snuggled between two crumb layers and baked. When cool, it is cut into squares or bars, although it is more fragile than a bar cookie.

Crumble — the British term for a crisp, if the topping includes oats.

Cobbler — sweetened and thickened fruit topped with sweet biscuit dough then baked. Sometimes a more flaky pie crust is used instead of the biscuit-like dough.

Pandowdy — generally made with apples and brown sugar or molasses, topped with a batter (either biscuit-like or a bread crumb topping), then baked until the top is crisp and crumbly.

Buckle — a simple white cake with fruit (usually blueberries) and a crumb topping.

Brown Betty — fruit layered and topped with a crumb mixture and baked. Sometimes custard is layered with the fruit. I wonder if Betty, whoever she was, knew her dessert would become an American classic?

THE BROADMOOR
COLORADO SPRINGS

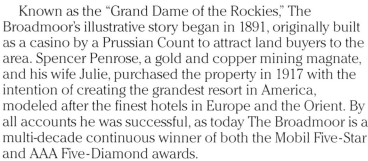

1 Lake Avenue
Colorado Springs, CO
80906
800.633.7711
www.thebroadmoor.com

Golf Courses:
East/West/Mountain

Designers: Donald Ross/
Robert Trent Jones, Sr./
Ed Seay & Arnold Palmer

Available holes: 45

Accommodations:
700 guestrooms,
including 107 suites

Rates: $$–$$$$

Other Activities: Spa,
tennis, hiking, horseback
riding, fly-fishing,
shopping

Known as the "Grand Dame of the Rockies," The Broadmoor's illustrative story began in 1891, originally built as a casino by a Prussian Count to attract land buyers to the area. Spencer Penrose, a gold and copper mining magnate, and his wife Julie, purchased the property in 1917 with the intention of creating the grandest resort in America, modeled after the finest hotels in Europe and the Orient. By all accounts he was successful, as today The Broadmoor is a multi-decade continuous winner of both the Mobil Five-Star and AAA Five-Diamond awards.

The mammoth Italian Renaissance-style stucco structures, clustered around an aesthetic man-made lake, seem just the right size for the surrounding Colorado Rocky Mountains, including the nearby 14,110-foot Pike's Peak. Three sculpted golf courses blanket the surrounding grounds, weaving in and out of forests of white pine, blue spruce, and giant hardwoods. At an elevation of just over 6,000 feet, the clean mountain air has an effect not only on golfers, but also on golf balls, which seem to travel farther in the thin air.

If the mountain stratosphere doesn't make you giddy, then the sheer number of dining options from which to choose might. From formal French to super-casual American sports fare, and several options in between, The Broadmoor serves up 10 different restaurants. The Penrose Room, a romantic setting with classic continental cuisine, tops the formal end of the scale and Charles Court, offering creative American and regional dishes, like Grilled Colorado Rack of Lamb, is resort casual. Café Julie, a quaint European-style bistro, is a guest favorite, as is Stratta's at the Golf Club, offering casual Italian dining in the evening and classic American club fare for breakfast and lunch. The following recipes represent the tempting feasts from Stratta's.

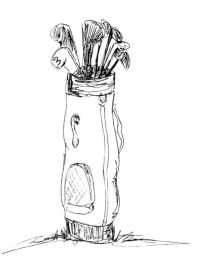

Breakfast Menu

- SUNRISE PARFAIT

- SOUTHWESTERN BREAKFAST BURRITO

- TAOS POTATOES

Dinner Menu

- BUTTERNUT SQUASH & GREEN PEA RISOTTO

- BISTECCA CON FUNGHI
  (FILET OF BEEF WITH FOREST MUSHROOMS)

SWEET POTATO FRITTATA

- BABA AU RHUM

- RECIPE INCLUDED

Golf Pro's Tip

Even with portions of the courses dating back to 1918, the management of shot placement is a premium, especially when hitting approach shots onto the greens. Never leave your ball where you are forced to putt away from the mountains, else you're guaranteed a very quick breaking putt.

Signature Hole

East course, Number 18, par 4 — the tee shot appears to head directly into the Rocky Mountains, followed by an approach shot over a small pond to a severely undulating green with the majestic Broadmoor Clubhouse in the background — a spectacular view from tee to green.

Sunrise Parfait

*L*ayered in a parfait or wineglass, this refreshing fruit, yogurt, and granola mix will dazzle even the sleepiest guest. You can assemble the parfait about an hour before you plan to serve it, but not much more than that or the granola will get soggy and the bananas will turn brown. You may, however, make the orange syrup and marinate the strawberries the night before to save time.

SERVES 4

1 cup water
½ cup sugar
¼ cup fresh squeezed orange juice
1 tablespoon Grand Marnier
   (optional)

1 pound fresh strawberries
1 large (8 ounces) banana
2 cups vanilla yogurt
8 tablespoons granola
4 springs fresh mint (garnish)

1. Place water, sugar, and orange juice in a saucepan over medium heat. Bring to a boil and reduce heat to a strong simmer.

2. Cook until mixture is reduced to a syrup consistency, about 10 minutes. Remove from heat and cool. Stir in Grand Marnier if using.

3. Pick out 4 beautiful strawberries and reserve as a garnish. Hull and slice enough of the remaining strawberries to equal 2 cups, about ¼-inch thick. Pour cooled syrup over sliced strawberries and let sit for 10 to 15 minutes.

4. Divide sliced strawberries with some of the juices between 4 red wine or parfait glasses.

5. Peel and slice banana into ¼-inch thick slices. Divide evenly between glasses, placing on top of strawberries.

6. Spoon in ½ cup yogurt on top of bananas in each glass. Top with 2 tablespoons of granola, a mint sprig, and a whole strawberry. Serve immediately, or chill up to 1 hour before serving.

Southwestern Breakfast Burrito

Southwestern food is my favorite food. Burritos for breakfast, how cool is that? Chorizo is pork sausage with garlic, mild or hot chile powder, and a little vinegar. You can find very mild chorizo that's still spicy with flavor, not heat. Sometimes the resort adds ½ cup cooked black beans to the filling for variation. You won't need to eat again for a while after this over-stuffed southwestern staple.

SERVES 2

6 ounces chorizo bulk sausage
1 tablespoon butter
2 tablespoons chopped green
   bell pepper
2 tablespoons chopped red bell
   pepper
2 tablespoons chopped red onion

4 eggs, beaten
2 large (10-inch) flour tortillas
½ cup shredded Monterey Jack
   cheese with peppers

Garnish:
Sour cream
Salsa

1. Heat the oven to 375°F. Brown chorizo in a skillet over medium heat until thoroughly cooked, about 8 to 10 minutes. Drain and set aside.

2. Wipe out skillet and melt the butter in it over medium heat. Stir in the peppers and onions. Sauté for a minute or so and then pour the beaten eggs over mixture.

3. Cook until eggs are set, gently stirring once or twice with a spatula, about 2 minutes.

4. While the eggs are cooking, place the tortillas on a sheet pan and sprinkle evenly with the cheese. Place in the oven to melt the cheese, about 2 minutes.

5. Stir the cooked chorizo into the eggs and heat thoroughly, about 1 minute.

6. Remove the tortillas from the oven when the cheese is melted, and place on a cutting board. Divide the egg mixture evenly between the tortillas, and roll from the bottom up, folding in the sides after the first fold. Cut in half at an angle.

7. Place on warm plates and garnish with sour cream and salsa.

Taos Potatoes

*T*he achiote paste is what makes these potatoes bear the name of Taos. Ground annatto seeds (which are also used to make butter yellow) are mixed with seasonings and an acid, like orange juice. The color is more dramatic than the flavor, turning the potatoes a lovely dusty orange color; the same color of the Taos adobe structures in the pre-dusk sun.

SERVES 6

3 large russet potatoes
(about 2¼ pounds)
2 tablespoons bacon drippings
1 cup chopped onion
½ cup chopped green bell pepper

½ cup chopped red bell pepper
1 tablespoon achiote paste*
1 tablespoon minced garlic
1½ teaspoons ground cumin
Salt and freshly ground white pepper

1. Peel potatoes and cut into ¾-inch cubes. Place in a steamer basket and steam for 10 minutes, or until partially cooked, still holding their shape but easily pierced with a fork. Spread on a baking sheet to dry. May be prepared 1 day in advance. After drying, store covered in the refrigerator.

2. Heat the bacon drippings in a large skillet over medium heat.

3. When skillet is hot, add the potatoes and onions, and cook until potatoes are just starting to turn brown, about 10 minutes, turning once or twice.

4. Stir in green and red bell peppers, achiote paste, garlic, and cumin. Cook until potatoes are done, about another 13 to 15 minutes. Season with salt and pepper.

I found achiote paste at A.J.'s Fine Foods near the spice section. Look for it in the Mexican food or spice section of your grocery store. Substitute with chile powder if you cannot locate achiote paste.

Turn up the heat: Add 1 or 2 chopped jalapeños to add throat-warming spice. Removing the seeds from the peppers will tone down the heat. Try this with serranos for even more kick.

Butternut Squash & Green Pea Risotto

*T*he Broadmoor serves this orange and green studded risotto in baked acorn squash rings. If you'd like to try that, see the note below. Whether you do the dramatic acorn presentation, or just serve the risotto in a pretty Italian bowl, the payoff is in the slight bite, the little resistance to the tooth, of each rich mouthful.

SERVES 5

3 tablespoons olive oil
½ cup chopped onion
½ teaspoon minced garlic
1¼ cups arborio rice
¼ cup dry vermouth or white wine
3 cups chicken or vegetable
    stock, hot
1¼ cups grated Parmesan
    cheese, divided
1 cup cooked peas

1 cup diced, cooked
    butternut squash*
¼ cup peeled, seeded, and
    chopped tomato
2 tablespoons lemon juice
1 tablespoon chopped basil (plus 10
    leaves for garnish)
Salt and freshly ground black pepper
½ cup toasted pine nuts**

1. Heat the olive oil in a saucepan over medium heat. Stir in the onions and garlic. Cook until onions are soft, about 3 minutes.

2. Stir in the rice, coating all the grains with oil. Cook another 2 minutes, stirring frequently.

3. Stir in vermouth or wine and let it mostly evaporate. Stir in ½ cup hot stock. Cook, stirring frequently, until rice absorbs stock. Repeat with remaining stock, letting each half-cup almost absorb before adding the next half-cup, stirring frequently. Check for doneness before adding the last half-cup. The rice should be porridge-like with some resistance when bitten (al dente). You may or may not need the last half-cup of stock. It should take about 18 to 20 minutes from the first to last addition of stock.

4. Fold in 1 cup of the Parmesan cheese. Fold in peas, squash, tomatoes, lemon juice, and chopped basil. Taste and season with salt and pepper.

5. Garnish with basil leaves, toasted pine nuts, and sprinkle with the remaining ¼ cup of Parmesan cheese.

Peel butternut squash, remove seeds, and cut into ¼-inch cubes. Using a mandoline or slicer helps create uniform cubes. Bring a pot of salted water to a boil. Boil squash for about 2 minutes, drain and plunge squash into ice water to stop the cooking. Spread on a sheet pan to dry. May be prepared 1 day in advance. Store covered in the refrigerator.

**To toast nuts, see page 19 under Common Procedures.*

NOTE: Heat oven to 350°F. Cut 1 acorn squash (about 1¼ pounds) into 1-inch crosswise rings. Scrape out seeds and place on a lined baking sheet. Sprinkle with a little brown sugar. Drizzle with a little orange juice and honey. Bake until tender, about 35 to 40 minutes. To serve, place a squash ring on a plate and mound the risotto in the center of the ring.

Bistecca con Funghi

Heated Plates!

Bistecca is Italian for beef steak, and this beef tenderloin is lusciously bathed in a deep red wine sauce, with earthy mushrooms and sweet roasted red peppers. The Broadmoor uses an Italian Barolo wine for the sauce, a full-bodied wine from the Piedmont region. Be sure to use portabella as part of the exotic mushroom mixture. Other good choices include shiitakes and chanterelles.

SERVES 6

- 6 (7-ounce) beef tenderloin filets
- 3 tablespoons olive oil
- 1 tablespoon minced garlic
- Salt and freshly ground black pepper
- 1 tablespoon butter
- 3 cups chopped exotic mushrooms
- 1 cup sliced roasted red bell peppers*
- 1 teaspoon fresh herbs (thyme, basil, rosemary, etc.)

need to be there

Sauce:

- 2 cups red wine (like Barolo or Chianti)
- 2 sprigs herbs (thyme, basil, rosemary, etc.)
- 1 cup demi-glace**

O. says 4/5

1. Marinate beef with olive oil and garlic at room temperature for 30 minutes, or up to 8 hours in the refrigerator. Meanwhile, make the sauce.

2. Bring red wine and herbs to a boil in a saucepan over medium-high heat. Vigorously boil until just 1/4 cup of liquid remains, about 15 to 20 minutes. Stir in demi-glace and cook to a sauce consistency, about another 5 minutes. Strain and season with salt and pepper. May be prepared 1 day in advance. Cool, then store covered in the refrigerator. Gently reheat before serving.

3. Heat a grill to medium-high heat (375° to 400°F). Season beef with salt and pepper. Grill to desired temperature, about 6 to 7 minutes per side for medium-rare. While steaks are grilling, prepare mushrooms and peppers.

4. Melt the butter in a skillet over medium heat. Stir in the mushrooms and cook until soft, about 5 minutes. Stir in roasted peppers and herbs. Heat through, another minute or so. Season with salt and pepper. Serve with steaks and wine sauce.

**To roast peppers, see page 18 under Common Procedures.*

***See Demi-glace under Common Procedures, page 17.*

more demi glace on steak non on potato

Nov. 8, 2003 Dinner Bill & Barb @ [illegible]

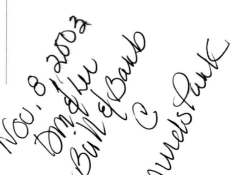

food combination ←

Sweet Potato Frittata

This crisp "frittata" is wonderful as a base for the previous Bistecca recipe. It also works well as a side dish to grilled chicken or pork, too. I like to rinse the onion in this recipe to remove some of its sharpness; otherwise I think it can overpower the sweet potato. You can prepare the other ingredients while the onions are soaking.

SERVES 6

½ cup finely chopped onion
1 pound sweet potatoes
½ pound russet potatoes
4 eggs
1½ teaspoons salt

¼ teaspoon nutmeg
¼ teaspoon ground white pepper
2 tablespoons chopped fresh herbs
    (thyme, basil, rosemary, etc.)
Vegetable oil

1. Soak onions in cold water for 5 minutes. Rinse and repeat once more.

2. Peel and shred sweet and russet potatoes. A food processor makes this quick and easy. Stir in drained onions.

3. Beat eggs with salt, nutmeg, white pepper, and herbs. Pour over potato mixture and toss until combined. Cover and place in the refrigerator for an hour.

4. Pour enough oil in a large skillet to come to ⅛-inch depth. Heat over medium heat until hot.

5. Scoop about ⅓ cup of potato mixture into hot oil (a #12 ice cream scoop is ⅓ cup). Cook 3 or 4 at a time, careful to not overcrowd the pan. Flatten with a spatula, and cook until golden brown on the bottom, about 5 minutes. Flip and brown the other side, another 4 minutes. Remove, blot with paper towels, then place on a sheet pan and keep warm in a 200°F oven while you finish the rest.

O-says o.k -
Don would have wanted more potato

delicious!
w/o demi glace
sort of over powered potatoes

Baba au Rhum

*T*his light, miniature yeast cake soaked in rum syrup makes an impressive statement. I have a pan specifically made for six miniature angel food cakes, and it's fine that two are empty come baking time. This cake is best served the day it's made. Fill the centers with vanilla pastry cream, as the resort does, or even with whipped cream or ice cream. I used the vanilla cream recipe on page 95. (See photograph on page P-2.)

SERVES 4

½ of a (.6-ounce) fresh yeast cake
⅓ cup plus 1 tablespoon (3 ounces) warm milk
1½ cups less 2 tablespoons flour
3 eggs
2 yolks
1½ teaspoons sugar
Pinch salt
8 tablespoons (1 stick) butter, softened and whipped

¾ cup sugar
½ cup water
2 to 3 tablespoons dark rum

Garnish:
Vanilla pastry cream (see page 95)
Fresh berries
Powdered sugar
Mint sprigs

1. Crumble yeast into the bowl of an electric mixer. Add the warm milk and whisk until the yeast dissolves. Stir enough of the measured flour (about ½ cup) in the yeast mixture to make a very loose dough. Sprinkle remaining flour on top of dough, but don't stir. Set aside to ferment until there are visible cracks on the flour surface, about 10 minutes.

2. Whisk the eggs, yolks, 1½ teaspoons of sugar, and salt together, then pour on top of flour mixture, and mix on low speed until almost smooth. Mix on medium speed for 10 minutes, stopping once to scrape down the sides and bottom of the bowl.

3. Mix in the whipped butter on low speed. Mix an additional 8 minutes on medium speed, stopping once to scrape sides and bottom.

4. Cover the dough and let rise until almost double in size, about 1 hour. Stir gently to expel excess gases. The dough will be very loose, like a very thick batter.

5. Spray 3-inch angel food cake molds with nonstick spray. Place dough in a large pastry bag with a large plain circle tip and pipe equal amounts into 4 molds, filling just under halfway. Let rise until double in size, about 35 to 45 minutes. Dough will be about 1-inch from top of mold but will rise during baking.

6. Heat oven to 400°F for 15 minutes. Place cake molds in center of the oven and bake until golden brown, about 12 to 14 minutes. Cool 2 to 3 minutes and remove from molds. Place babas in a shallow pan. While babas are baking, make the rum syrup in step 7.

7. Stir the ¾ cup sugar and ½ water together in a small saucepan. Heat over medium heat and stir just until sugar dissolves. Cool slightly and stir in rum. Pour over babas, coating each one. Soak for 15 minutes. Drain, reserving liquid.

8. To serve, turn babas upside down on a dessert plate. Pipe pastry cream into the center. Drizzle remaining syrup over babas. Scatter a few berries around the plate and sprinkle with powdered sugar. Finish with a sprig of mint.

BABA AU RHUM
VS. SAVARIN

Baba au Rhum is purportedly the result of a 17th century Polish King soaking his stale kugelhopf cake in rum. Kugelhopf is an Eastern European rich but light yeast cake often containing dried fruits such as raisins and apricots. Did the King name his new creation after the *Ali Baba and the Forty Thieves* fairy-tale hero or after a similar Polish word for "grandmother"? No one knows for sure.

Tall cylindrical molds are used to bake the dessert, and the mini-angel food cake molds I used for the preceding recipe resemble baba molds, though they are not quite as tall. If the cake is baked sans raisins in a large ring mold, it's called a savarin. Both are generally filled with vanilla pastry cream.

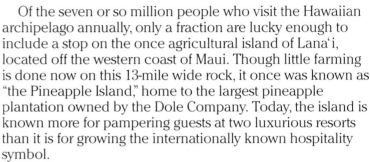

P.O. Box 630310
Lana'i City, Hawaii 96763
800.321.4666
www.islandoflanai.com

Golf Courses: The
Experience at Koele

Designers: Greg Norman
& Ted Robinson

Available holes: 18

Accommodations:
102 guestrooms,
including suites

Rates: $$$–$$$$

Other Activities: tennis,
croquet, swimming,
horseback riding,
sporting clays, archery,
hiking, mountain biking

Of the seven or so million people who visit the Hawaiian archipelago annually, only a fraction are lucky enough to include a stop on the once agricultural island of Lana'i, located off the western coast of Maui. Though little farming is done now on this 13-mile wide rock, it once was known as "the Pineapple Island," home to the largest pineapple plantation owned by the Dole Company. Today, the island is known more for pampering guests at two luxurious resorts than it is for growing the internationally known hospitality symbol.

Travel inland from the shore and step back in time at the Lodge at Koele, an upcountry resort resembling a plantation house of yesteryear. The property sits high in the middle of the island, surrounded by Cook Island pines and eucalyptus trees. The nights can be cool, even at an elevation of 1,600 feet. Most evenings, a fire crackles in the stone fireplace in the grand living area, the perfect spot to retreat after an artful meal, blending game, seafood, and tropical ingredients. Rich colors, wooden floors, rattan armchairs, and overstuffed sofas invite guests to linger well into the evening.

Jackets are required for the Formal Dining Room, where the chef features daily catches from the surrounding waters, island wild venison, tropical fruits, and vegetables from local gardens. The Terrace Room offers a more casual dining option, with decidedly mainland items enhanced with tropical touches. Pan-fried pumpkin ravioli might share the menu with pineapple-kissed crab cakes. The Clubhouse Bar & Grill serves traditional food for golfers (burgers and club sandwiches) along with a few Asian-inspired appetizers such as island pork spring rolls and duck and ginger won tons.

Dinner Menu

SPICY POACHED ASIAN PEAR ON ISLAND GREENS

• ROAST VENISON (OR PORK)
WITH MADEIRA SAUCE & APPLE MANGO RELISH

• CARAMELIZED MAUI ONION RISOTTO

COCONUT CRÈME BRÛLÉE

• *Recipe included*

Golf Pro's Tip

Trade winds often pick up speed on the island, especially in the afternoon, making golfing into the wind an unavoidable challenge. Practice a low-flying "punch shot" to get the ball onto the green.

Signature Hole

The Experience at Koele, Number 17, par 4 — dramatic 250-foot drop from elevated tee to green bordered by a lake on right side, and mist-covered dense shrubs along the left.

Roast Venison (or Pork)

WITH MADEIRA SAUCE

*W*ild venison is a star in many dishes at the Lodge at Koele, including this simple but flavor-packed recipe. I tested it with pork as well, and my tasters were just as happy with the results (some liked it better than the farm-raised venison I used.). The difference is in the cooking time. The pork will take just a bit longer than the venison, because you want the pork to be at least medium internal temperature (145° to 150°F) and venison tastes best at medium-rare (130° to 140°F). The fruit relish (see next recipe) adds bright tangy notes that complement the deep, rich flavored sauce. (See photograph on page P-3.)

SERVES 4 TO 6

1½ pounds venison (or pork)
 tenderloins
¼ cup olive oil
2 teaspoons minced garlic
2 teaspoons fresh thyme leaves

Salt and freshly ground black pepper
1 cup Madeira
1 sprig fresh thyme
1¼ cups demi-glace*

1. Marinate tenderloins in olive oil, garlic, and thyme leaves at room temperature for 30 minutes, or up to 4 hours in the refrigerator, bringing to room temperature before proceeding. Heat the oven to 400°F after marinating the meat.

2. Bring the Madeira to boil over medium-high heat in a tall saucepan. Reduce liquid to roughly 3 tablespoons, about 8 to 10 minutes. Stir in the sprig of thyme and demi-glace. Return to a boil, then reduce heat and simmer for about 5 minutes. Season with salt and pepper. Sauce may be made 1 day in advance. Cool, then store covered in the refrigerator. Gently reheat before serving.

3. Heat an ovenproof skillet over high heat. Drain tenderloins and season with salt and pepper. Sear on all sides until brown, about 6 minutes total. Place pan in the oven and roast until desired temperature, about 9 minutes for medium-rare (130°F) and about 15 minutes for medium (145°F). Remove from oven and cover with foil. Rest 5 minutes before slicing at an angle to serve.

See Demi-glace under Common Procedures, page 17.

Apple Mango Relish

Colorful and tangy, sweet and spicy, this condiment is a wonderful companion to many meat dishes, including the previous recipe. The ginger, jalapeño, and red pepper flakes give it a nice kick. Remove the jalapeño seeds if you prefer not to be kicked. The best part about this relish is that you can make it in advance and it keeps for a week.

MAKES 2 CUPS

1 tablespoon olive oil
¼ cup chopped onion
1 tablespoon peeled and grated
   fresh ginger
¼ cup peeled, cored, and chopped
   apple
⅓ cup dried cranberries
¼ cup water
¼ cup rice wine vinegar

¼ cup sugar
1 star anise pod
1 stick of cinnamon (or pinch of
   ground cinnamon)
1 mango, peeled and chopped
   (about 1 cup)
1 tablespoon minced jalapeño
Pinch of red pepper flakes

1. Heat the olive oil in a saucepan over medium heat. Cook onions until fragrant, about 1 minute. Stir in ginger, apple, and cranberries. Cook, stirring frequently, for another minute.

2. Stir in water, vinegar, sugar, and spices. Bring to a boil, reduce heat, and simmer until thick and syrupy, about 10 to 12 minutes.

3. Stir in mango, jalapeño, and pepper flakes. Cook another minute or two. Remove star anise pod and cinnamon stick. Serve warm or at room temperature. Store covered in the refrigerator, up to 1 week.

Maui Onion Risotto

*C*aramelized onions are sweet and crunchy, and worth every minute it takes to properly caramelize them. You can make the onions a day or two in advance, and then this risotto is doable even on weeknights, as long as you don't mind staying close to the stove to stir. If you can't find Maui onions, any sweet variety will do, such as Vadalia, Walla Walla, Texas 1015's, or Oso Sweet.

SERVES 4 TO 6

2 tablespoon olive oil
3 large Maui or other sweet onions
  (about 1½ pounds), thinly sliced
1 tablespoon roasted garlic*
1 cup dry white wine
1¼ cups arborio rice
2 teaspoons fresh thyme leaves

½ cup finely chopped chives
3 cups chicken or vegetable
  stock, hot
¼ cup heavy cream
½ cup grated Parmesan cheese
Salt and freshly ground white pepper

1. Heat olive oil in a large skillet over medium heat. Stir in onions and roasted garlic. Cook slowly, stirring frequently, until onions are lightly caramelized, about 45 minutes.

2. Stir in wine and simmer until most of the liquid has evaporated, about 10 minutes.

3. Stir in rice and fresh herbs. Cook, stirring frequently, for a couple of minutes.

4. Pour in ½ cup hot stock, and cook, stirring frequently, as the rice absorbs the liquid. Stir in another half-cup of stock, letting the rice absorb the liquid before adding the next half-cup, repeat with 2 more half-cup additions. Check for doneness before adding the last half-cup. The rice should be porridge-like with some resistance when bitten (al dente). You may or may not need the last half-cup. It should take about 18 to 20 minutes from the first to the last addition of stock.

5. Stir in the heavy cream and reduce until thick and creamy, about 2 minutes, stirring occasionally. Stir in Parmesan cheese. Season with salt and white pepper.

To roast garlic, see page 18 under Common Procedures

THE ART
OF RISOTTO

A good risotto is thick, creamy, and almost porridge-like, with plump grains of rice that offer just the slightest resistance when bitten — al dente, as the Italians say. The trick is in the technique. First, sauté the rice in a little butter or olive oil, then slowly stir in hot stock, a little at a time so that the rice absorbs it before adding more liquid. Sautéing the rice coaxes the starch from the grains to begin the cooking process. The slow and gradual addition of hot liquid allows the starch to thicken without drowning the rice, thus creating the creamy texture. The process can take anywhere from 20 to 25 minutes, with constant attention. It's worth the time it takes and the attention you give it, stirring the rice gently between stock additions. The reward is apparent in the first bite—rich, creamy rice with a lovely texture.

Choosing the correct rice is important to the success of risotto. The rice needs to have a high starch content, and be tough enough to stand up to a constant stir. Regular long-grain white rice just doesn't have enough starch to make risotto. Arborio rice is the most common rice used in making risotto in the U.S., and is widely available in most grocery stores today, though it wasn't always the case. There are many varieties of risotto-style rice, but most are available only in Italy. Two other Italian risotto rice varieties available in our country that make beautiful risottos are *Baldo* and *Carnaroli*. You might have to search these out in a specialty grocery store, or on the Internet. Many restaurant chefs prefer the more costly Carnaroli over arborio. Carnaroli is expensive because it is more difficult to grow and yields less rice per square foot than other rice varieties. The grains are slightly smaller than arborio grains. Some chefs say the end result is a softer, creamier risotto. I've cooked with both and feel either rice will produce a memorable risotto if the proper technique is followed.

P.O. Box 630310
Lana'i City, Hawaii 96763
800.321.4666
www.islandoflanai.com

Golf Courses:
Challenge at Manele

Designer: Jack Nicklaus

Available holes: 18

Accommodations:
250 guestrooms,
including suites

Rates: $$$–$$$$

Other Activities: Spa,
tennis, swimming,
Hawaiian crafts,
snorkeling, diving, sea
kayaking, and boating

Perched just above the pure white sand of Hulopo'e Beach, the expansive Manele Bay Hotel hugs the southern coastline of the island of Lana'i. It is a sprawling collection of Mediterranean and Asian influenced structures with sun-bleached white walls and angled blue tile roofs. A gorgeous pristine pool begs you to leave the open-air lobby, filled with ornate Far East antiques and plush oriental rugs, guiding you toward the turquoise sea.

Compared to its sister resort, the rural Lodge at Koele (see previous chapter), the Manele Bay Hotel feels cosmopolitan, almost formal, even as guests in Bermuda shorts and silk floral shirts lazily lounge on the brightly colored sofas scattered throughout the palatial split-level lobby.

Dining in the formal Ihilani Restaurant reveals the successful fusion of Mediterranean-Hawaiian influences. The chef creatively intertwines Mediterranean presentations with the freshest Hawaiian ingredients, presenting showstoppers like pan-seared sea scallops with vegetable couscous and grilled yellowfin tuna with shaved Manchego cheese.

Hulopo'e Court, the all-day dining room located on the east side of the lower lobby, uses the dinner menu to showcase regional Hawaiian cuisine. Warm calamari with spicy cabbage slaw and tamarind dressing might start a meal of citrus grilled tiger prawns or spice-rubbed chicken with mango sauce.

The Clubhouse Restaurant at the golf course just west of the main hotel, serves pupus (pronounced poo-poo's), Hawaiian-style appetizers featuring island-inspired fare from the garden (vine-ripened tomato salad with shaved sweet onion), the land (glazed pork ribs with Asian slaw) and sea (ahi sashimi with fresh wasabi).

Nov. 8 2003

W/Lu, Brady, Bill, Barb @ Munds Park

"A KEEPER"

Dinner Menu

- Coconut Lime Hearts of Palm Salad

  Warm Calamari with
- Pineapple Tamarind Spicy Cabbage Slaw

- Hamachi Tartare with Coconut and Cilantro

- Twice-Cooked Plantains

  Pineapple Sorbet in a Coconut Tuile

- *Recipe included*

Don said "He just did it the way "he" told me"

Golf Pro's Tip

Driving the ball well is the key to scoring well at the Challenge at Manele. Some of the tee shots seem intimidating, but the fairways are much wider in the landing areas, leaving you plenty of room to play the next shot.

Signature Hole

Challenge at Manele, Number 12, par 3 — demanding tee shot from 150-foot cliff crosses over crashing ocean waves to a green that's larger than it appears. Bring an extra ball.

Coconut Lime Hearts of Palm Salad

*W*onderful tropical flavors shine through on this gorgeous salad. After you see the photograph on page P-4, the plate presentation instructions below will make more sense. The resort has access to fresh hearts of palm, but the canned variety works just fine. Hothouse cucumbers are also called English cucumbers, though most of the ones available in the market are from Mexico. They have thinner skins and less pronounced seeds than the typical garden-variety cucumber.

SERVES 4

Hearts of Palm Salad:
20 asparagus spears, trimmed
5 ounces (about 8 cups) mixed
   baby greens
1 (14.5-ounce) can hearts of palm,
   drained and rinsed
½ hothouse cucumber
¼ cup chopped toasted
   macadamia nuts*

Coconut Lime Dressing:
½ cup coconut milk
¼ cup rice wine vinegar
2 tablespoons lime juice
2 tablespoons honey
¾ cup vegetable oil
Salt and freshly ground black pepper

1. Bring a pot of salted water to a boil and prepare a large bowl of ice water. Gently boil asparagus until bright green and just barely tender, about 1 to 3 minutes, depending upon thickness. Strain and dunk spears in ice cold water to stop the cooking process. When cool, about 5 minutes, remove and pat dry. Meanwhile, make vinaigrette.

2. Whisk (or purée in a blender) the first 4 vinaigrette ingredients (coconut milk through honey) together or blend in a blender. Slowly drizzle in oil while whisking (or with the blender running). Season with salt and pepper. May be made 1 day in advance. Store covered in the refrigerator.

3. Toss greens with 3 to 4 tablespoons of dressing. Mound 2 cups of greens toward the back of 4 chilled salad plates.

4. Arrange 5 or 6 asparagus spears per plate, tips resting up at an angle on the greens and stems pointing down in front of the greens.

5. Cut the hearts of palm in half lengthwise, then in half again lengthwise to create long spears. Lay 5 or 6 spears on top of the asparagus spears, in the same direction.

6. Using a vegetable peeler, slice thin lengthwise strips of cucumber from the cucumber half, making thin ribbons. Curl several ribbons on one side of the plate to the side of the asparagus and hearts of palm spears.

7. Pour a tiny pool of dressing on the front of the plate in front of the asparagus. Sprinkle this pool with a tablespoon of chopped macadamia nuts. Drizzle any remaining dressing on the cucumber ribbons. This makes a beautiful salad. See picture on page P-4.

To toast nuts, see page 18 under Common Procedures.

The Lodge at Pebble Beach

Crab Cakes with Citrus Aïoli & Fennel & Endive Slaw
White Plate Special

The Broadmoor

Baba au Rhum

The Lodge at Koele

Roast Venison with Madeira &
Apple Mango Chutney

Coconut Lime Hearts
of Palm Salad

Manele Bay Hotel

Hamachi Tartare on
Twice-Cooked Plantains

Bandon Dunes

Vanilla-Crusted French Toast

The Boulders

Blue Corn Pancakes

*The Fairmont
Scottsdale
Princess*

*Rock Shrimp
Strudel
with Yellow
Sun-Dried
Tomato Sauce*

The Lodge at Ventana Canyon

*Black & White Napoleon
with Fresh Berries*

Spicy Cabbage Slaw
WITH PINEAPPLE TAMARIND DRESSING

*T*amarind paste is the color of molasses, and is used extensively in Asian, Middle Eastern, and Mexican cuisines. This sweet and sour condiment is also an important ingredient in Worcestershire sauce. I found individual packets of tamarind paste in the Mexican food aisle of my regular grocery store. It likely will have a large seed or two that is too sticky to remove. That's fine because you'll strain it later. The resort tops this slaw with calamari (squid) fried in a light cornstarch batter. I think it's also the perfect accompaniment to grilled teriyaki chicken or shrimp.

SERVES 5

Pineapple Dressing:
2 tablespoons pineapple juice
1 tablespoon tamarind paste
½ teaspoon red or green Thai
   curry paste
¼ cup honey
½ cup vegetable oil
Salt and freshly ground black pepper

Cabbage Slaw:
2 cups thinly sliced napa (Chinese) or
   green cabbage
2 cups thinly sliced red cabbage
¼ cup chopped fresh mint leaves
¼ cup thinly sliced green onions
¼ cup thinly sliced red radishes
Salt and freshly ground black pepper

To make dressing:

1. Heat juice, tamarind, and curry paste in a small saucepan over low heat. Simmer until tamarind dissolves, about 3 minutes.

2. Stir in honey and heat until dissolved. Remove from heat and strain to remove tamarind seed(s).

3. Slowly whisk oil into tamarind mixture. Use a blender for a thick, creamy dressing. Season with salt and pepper to taste. Cool.

To make slaw:

1. Toss all ingredients with ⅓ cup of dressing (more or less depending upon your particular taste).

2. Season with salt and pepper. The salad is best eaten as soon as it's dressed. The dressing will keep covered in the refrigerator, up to 3 days.

Hamachi Tartare

with Coconut and Cilantro

···

*N*ow don't go turning your nose up because you think this is raw fish. It is, but that's not the point. The point is that it's good and it doesn't taste like raw fish with the yummy coconut milk, tart lime juice, and crunchy sweet onion. Of course, you need to start with a really good quality fish. Hamachi is young yellowtail, found in the Pacific, with a firm texture similar to tuna. Sashimi grade ahi (yellowfin tuna) works well, too. The chef at Manele Bay serves this on top of twice-cooked plantains (see next recipe and photograph on page P-4).

Serves 5

2 tablespoons coconut milk
2 tablespoons chopped cilantro
2 tablespoons minced sweet onion
   (like Maui)
1 tablespoon seeded and minced
   red jalapeño
Juice of ½ lime (about 1 tablespoon)
Salt and freshly ground black pepper

½ pound cold skinless hamachi
   (young yellowtail) or ahi
   (yellowfin tuna)

Garnish:
2 tablespoons fresh cilantro leaves
5 lime slices
½ cup chopped red bell pepper

1. Whisk first 5 ingredients (coconut milk through lime juice) together. Season with salt and pepper to taste.

2. Chop fish into small chunks, about the size of peas.

3. Toss coconut mixture with fish. Let sit 5 minutes, but no more than 15 minutes before serving.

4. To serve, mound a little marinated fish in the center of the plate (or on top of a twice-cooked plantain (see next recipe). Garnish with cilantro, lime slices and chopped red bell pepper.

NOTE: Do not save any leftovers. Mishandled raw fish can cause severe food-borne illnesses.

Twice-Cooked Plantains

*I*f you love potatoes, I think you will enjoy these starchy flat disks made from a variety of bananas meant for cooking. Green plantains are best for this dish. As they ripen and turn from yellow to brown to black, the starch begins to convert to sugar and is less desirable for this preparation. The resort serves these plantain cakes as the base for the Hamachi Tartare. I think they're also delicious as a side to hoisin-barbecued ribs.

SERVES 5

2 cups peanut or vegetable oil
3 (8 to 10 ounces each) green plantains

Salt and freshly ground
  black pepper

1. Heat the oil in a deep pot to 350°F.

2. Cut lengthwise incisions through the skin of the plantain with a sharp knife. Peel off skin and cut plantains crosswise into 1-inch sections, at a slight angle.

3. In batches, gently lower plantains into hot oil with a heatproof slotted spoon and fry until golden brown, turning to brown all sides, about 2 minutes. Remove plantains with the slotted spoon and drain on paper towels. Repeat with remaining pieces. Keep oil hot.

4. Cover plantains with plastic wrap and using a small, heavy pot or a mallet, gently pound to flatten out to ¼-inch thickness.

5. Again in batches, return flattened plantains to hot oil and fry until crisp, about 1 to 2 minutes per side. Remove with the slotted spoon and drain of fresh paper towels. Quickly season with salt and pepper while hot. Serve immediately.

BANDON DUNES
golf resort

57744 Round Lake Drive
Bandon, OR 97411
888.345.6008
www.bandondunes.com

Golf Courses:
Bandon Dunes/
Pacific Dunes

Designers: David McLay
Kidd/Tom Doak

Available holes: 36

Accommodations:
153 guestrooms,
including suites

Rates: $–$$$$

Other Activities:
Guided angling trips,
eco-trails, horseback
riding, sea kayaking

It's all about golf at this relatively new resort (1999), secluded along the rugged southern Oregon coast, a good four hours from Portland. Bandon Dunes was built for serious golf lovers — not necessarily for the best golfers despite the difficult layout, but certainly for those who have a love of the game that goes beyond the casual weekend affair. Much ado has already been made about how this course is truer to its Scottish Links intentions than other courses claiming the same fame. Indeed, a young Scot did design the resort's first course. Those that have made the pilgrimage to Bandon Dunes boast that the seaside course is an honorable tribute to the game's roots.

Though the ocean is in view on all 18 holes of the Bandon Dunes course, it's the seven cliff-top holes hugging the coastline that catch the breath in the throat just as surely as the wind halts the ball in midair. Both Bandon Dunes and Pacific Dunes are walking courses, and caddies are highly recommended, at least for the first time outing. Another nod to the seriousness of golf at this remote haven is the 32-acre practice center, where golfers may practice every shot needed on either of the two courses before stepping onto the real thing. The center is designed to make use of every club in the bag, with a long range, a short range, a 1- acre practice putting green, and a large bunker area for those inevitable sand shots.

Between practicing and playing, make time to sample the hearty Pacific Northwest cuisine served in the main lodge. Duck with Cranberry Barbecue Sauce shares the menu with the chef's grandmother's tasty meatloaf as well as local wild King salmon. The food is not fussy — just straightforward and there is plenty of it, much like the golf.

Breakfast Menu

- CRANBERRY ORANGE SCONES

- VANILLA-CRUSTED FRENCH TOAST WITH FRESH BERRIES

Dinner Menu

- THAI COCONUT MUSSELS

- PAN-SEARED BREAST OF CHICKEN WITH SOY GINGER GLAZE
AND SAIFUN NOODLES
OR
- DOUBLE-CUT GRILLED PORK CHOP WITH APPLE PEAR
HABAÑERO CHUTNEY
OR
- GRANDMA THAYER'S GLAZED MEATLOAF

- CHALLAH BREAD PUDDING WITH CARROT CRÈME ANGLAISE

- *Recipe included*

Golf Pro's Tip

Keep your golf ball low for two reasons. One, you can bump-and-run your ball onto most of the greens, much like the courses in Scotland and Ireland. Two, when it's breezy (which is often) a low shot is usually a more productive shot.

Signature Hole

Bandon Dunes course, Number 5 — captivating par 4 with the Pacific on the left, sandy dunes all around, and a fairway split by tufts of beach grass, this slender hole plays directly into the wind.

Cranberry Orange Scones

Tender, light, and bursting with cranberries and orange zest, this simple scone recipe takes very little time and effort and the rewards are sweet and satisfying.

SERVES 8

2 cups flour
3 tablespoons sugar
1 tablespoon baking powder
½ teaspoon salt
1 egg, lightly beaten

⅔ cup heavy cream
6 tablespoons butter, melted
½ cup dried cranberries
1 tablespoon orange zest

1. Heat oven to 425°F. Whisk first 4 ingredients together (flour through salt).

2. Whisk egg and cream together, and fold mixture into flour. When almost combined stir in melted butter. Fold in cranberries and zest, careful to not overmix. The dough will be very sticky.

3. Line a baking sheet with parchment paper or a silicone mat. Scrape dough onto baking sheet and with floured hands, pat into an 8-inch disk, about 1-inch thick. Cut into 8 wedges with a knife, but don't separate the wedges.

4. Bake until light golden brown, about 12 to 14 minutes.

Vanilla-Crusted French Toast

*S*inful! And you are worth every bite. Crunchy French toast is a two-step process: first, cooking over a relatively moderate heat for a golden crust, and second, finishing the toast in a hot oven. Get creative if you want by changing the flavor of the ice cream. Strawberry works very well. Melt the ice cream in the refrigerator overnight. (See photograph on page P-5.)

SERVES 4 TO 6

1 pint premium vanilla ice cream, melted
4 egg yolks
12 slices challah bread (about 1 loaf), cut into 1-inch thick slices

4 cups crushed corn flakes
1 tablespoon vegetable oil
1 cup fresh mixed berries for garnish
Warm maple syrup

1. Heat the oven to 375°F. Heat a large griddle or nonstick skillet over medium-low heat.

2. Beat melted ice cream with egg yolks. (Don't even think about it.)

3. Dip bread slices in batter, then roll in corn flakes. Set in a shallow baking pan to soak for a minute while you dip a few more.

4. Brush griddle or skillet with a thin coat of oil and fry the toast until brown, about 2 to 3 minutes, flip and cook the other side until brown, about 2 more minutes. Set an ovenproof cooling rack in the oven. (Place another baking sheet on the rack below to catch crumbs.) Place browned toast on the rack and bake for 5 minutes, until the outside is crispy and the interior is done. (A baking sheet doesn't work as well as a rack because the hot air doesn't reach the bottom of the toast on a baking sheet.)

5. Serve with fresh berries and warm maple syrup.

Thai Coconut Mussels

*T*he coconut broth is coyly sweet and a bit spicy — a perfect pool for plump, juicy, indigo blue mussels. A couple of ingredients are worth seeking out at an Asian specialty market, but don't despair if you can't find the kaffir lime leaves or fresh lemongrass stalks. You can still make and enjoy this dish without these two mild citrus-floral ingredients by replacing them with a teaspoon of lime zest and a teaspoon of lime juice. Although that's not a true indication of what these delicate ingredients taste like, it's better than skipping this delightful dish altogether.

SERVES 4 TO 6

1 tablespoon vegetable oil
½ cup (about 3 ounces) peeled and finely chopped fresh ginger
½ cup finely chopped onion
1 teaspoon minced garlic
1 stalk (about 1 ounce) fresh lemongrass, cut into 1-inch pieces
2 kaffir lime leaves
½ teaspoon dried thyme
1 teaspoon red Thai curry paste
¼ cup white wine
1 small (6 ounces) sweet potato, peeled and chopped into ½-inch cubes

½ cup brown sugar
1 cup chicken stock
¼ cup water
2 teaspoons red chile flakes
2 pounds live common mussels
1 (14.5-ounce) can coconut milk

Garnish:
1 lime cut into wedges
4 tablespoons fresh chopped cilantro
2 tablespoons fresh chopped basil

1. Heat olive oil in a saucepan over medium heat. Stir in ginger, onions, and garlic. Smash the lemongrass pieces with a meat mallet until flat and splintery, and add to the saucepan along with the kaffir lime leaves and dried thyme. Cook, stirring occasionally, until onions are soft, about 3 to 4 minutes.

2. Stir in curry paste, coating all the ingredients, then stir in the white wine. Cook until wine evaporates, about a minute.

3. Stir in sweet potatoes, brown sugar, chicken stock, water, and chile flakes. Bring to a boil, then reduce heat to a simmer. Cook until liquid reduces by half, about 15 to 20 minutes.

4. While liquid is reducing in step 3, place mussels in large pot and set under cold running water for 15 minutes to help the mussels expel any sand.

5. Strain the reduced broth into another saucepan large enough to hold the mussels. Stir the coconut milk into the strained liquid. Bring the coconut broth up to poaching temperature, about 170°F, (barely simmering) over medium heat, then reduce heat to low to maintain the poaching temperature.

6. Scrub the mussels with a brush, removing the stringy beard and discarding any that are cracked, chipped, or don't close when tapped lightly.

7. Add the cleaned mussels to the broth. Gently stir and cover. Poach until mussels open up and are done, about 8 to 10 minutes. Discard any mussels that do not open. Serve mussels with broth in warm bowls and garnish with lime wedges, cilantro, and basil.

Pan-Seared Breast of Chicken
WITH SOY GINGER GLAZE

*H*ere's a quick and flavorful glaze for chicken that also works well on pork. The resort fries up some bean thread (saifun) noodles as a garnish for this dish. This recipe calls for chile paste. Any brand will do, even chile sauce, instead of paste, if that's what you have on hand. You'll find several varieties on the Asian food aisle of most grocery stores.

SERVES 6

Soy Ginger Glaze:
1 cup hoisin sauce
3 tablespoons brown sugar
3 tablespoons soy sauce
2 tablespoons sherry
1 tablespoon peeled and grated
   fresh ginger
2 teaspoons minced garlic
½ to 1 teaspoon chile paste
1½ teaspoons dark sesame oil
Pinch dry ground ginger

Chicken:
1 tablespoon oil (preferably peanut)
6 (7-ounce) skinned, boned chicken
   breast halves
Salt and freshly ground black pepper
½ cup thinly sliced green onions

1. Whisk glaze ingredients (hoisin through dry ginger) together and set aside.

2. Heat oven to 350°F. Heat oil in an oven-proof skillet over medium-high heat until very hot. Season chicken breasts with salt and pepper. Sear chicken until golden brown on both sides, about 3 minutes per side.

3. Pour ½ cup of glaze into a small bowl and brush on chicken breasts. Discard this used glaze and wash brush. Finish cooking breasts in the oven until done (internal temperature 160°F), about 12 to 14 minutes. Brush breasts with remaining glaze using a clean brush. Top with sliced green onions.

Double-Cut Grilled Pork Chop

WITH APPLE PEAR HABAÑERO CHUTNEY

*B*utterflied chops are cut from double-cut chops, which just means double-thickness, or 2 bones per chop. You really want the meat before it's cut into a butterfly. Ask your butcher, and try to get chops with bones, as they impart more flavor to the meat.

SERVES 6

6 (10-ounce) double-cut pork chops,
  with bones
2 tablespoons olive oil

Salt and freshly ground black pepper
Apple Pear Habañero Chutney
  (recipe follows)

1. Heat the grill to medium-high (375° to 400°F). Brush chops with olive oil and sprinkle with salt and pepper.

2. Grill on both sides until medium, (145° to 150°F), about 20 to 25 minutes total. You can put diamond (cross-hatch) grill marks on the chops by placing the chops on a hot grill for 5 minutes, then rotating the chop (same side down) about a quarter turn and grilling another 5 minutes before flipping to cook the other side.

3. Remove from grill and rest 5 minutes before serving. Serve on a warm plate with a dollop of chutney.

Apple Pear Habañero Chutney

*H*abañeros are at the top of the heat scale, so exercise extreme caution when handling these tiny, colorful, pumpkin-shaped peppers. Wear those latex disposable kitchen gloves you have stashed in your drawer. Substitute a jalapeño or the slightly hotter serrano chile if you think the habañero might be too hot for you, although with just a teaspoon and the seeds removed, it's not too hot to handle.

MAKES 3 CUPS

1 cup cider vinegar
1 cup chopped onion
2 medium green apples, peeled, cored, and chopped (about 2½ cups)
2 medium ripe pears, peeled, cored, and chopped (about 2 cups)
1½ cups sugar
1 tablespoon whole mustard seed
1 tablespoon peeled and grated fresh ginger
2 teaspoons minced garlic

1 teaspoon seeded and minced habañero chile
½ teaspoon dry ground ginger
¼ teaspoon ground coriander
¼ teaspoon ground cumin
¼ teaspoon anise seed
¼ teaspoon cinnamon
⅛ teaspoon ground nutmeg
2 tablespoons arrowroot or cornstarch
2 tablespoons cold water

1. Heat vinegar, onions, apples, and pears in a saucepan over medium heat. Bring to a boil, then reduce to a strong simmer, cooking until vinegar reduces to ¼ cup, about 5 minutes.

2. Stir in the next 11 ingredients (sugar through nutmeg). Cook gently until fruit is tender but not mushy, about 3 minutes.

3. Bring mixture to a full boil. Whisk arrowroot with cold water and stir into boiling chutney. Reduce heat to simmer, and cook for another minute or so.

4. Serve warm or at room temperature. May be prepared up to 3 days in advance. Store covered in the refrigerator.

Grandma Thayer's Glazed Meatloaf

*A*ren't we always looking for that perfect meatloaf recipe? This one is special for two reasons. One, it really is a personal family recipe from the chef's grandmother. Two, it packs a flavorful punch from lots of aromatic vegetables and a combination of different meats. You might want to double the recipe if you're a fan of those day-after meatloaf sandwiches.

SERVES 6

1 tablespoon olive oil
1 cup finely chopped onion
½ cup finely chopped celery
½ cup finely chopped carrot
1 tablespoon minced garlic
1 tablespoon minced shallots
1 cup fresh white bread crumbs*
1 egg yolk
4 tablespoons butter, cut into
   tiny pieces
2 tablespoons heavy cream
1 tablespoon Worcestershire sauce
1 teaspoon dried thyme

1 teaspoon hot pepper sauce
1½ teaspoons salt
½ teaspoon freshly ground
   black pepper
1 pound ground beef
½ pound ground pork
½ pound ground veal

Meatloaf Glaze:
½ cup ketchup
1 tablespoon brown sugar
1 tablespoon prepared yellow mustard

1. Heat oven to 350°F. Heat olive oil in a large skillet. Stir in onions, celery, carrots, garlic, and shallots. Cook until onions are soft, about 3 or 4 minutes. Remove from heat and cool.

2. Pour cooled onion mixture into a large bowl and stir in the next 9 ingredients (bread crumbs through black pepper). Thoroughly mix in the beef, pork, and veal.

3. Transfer the mixture to a standard loaf pan and smooth the top. Bake for 30 minutes.

4. Whisk the meatloaf glaze ingredients together until the brown sugar dissolves. Spread the glaze over the top of the meatloaf and bake another 15 minutes, or until done.

The easiest way to get fresh bread crumbs is to pulse torn bread pieces in a food processor. You need about 3 slices of white bread, crusts removed, to yield 1 cup of crumbs.

Challah Bread Pudding
WITH CARROT CRÈME ANGLAISE

*T*he drier the bread the better in this dish. I cut the bread into cubes and let them dry on a sheet pan on the counter the day before I make this dessert. You could lightly toast them in a 350°F oven for about 5 minutes instead. Either way, the egg-rich bread soaked in the almond and spice cream bakes up crispy on top and tender inside, and is just as good chilled, as it is warm.

SERVES 8 TO 10

5 cups heavy cream
5 egg yolks
1½ cups sugar
2 tablespoons (1 ounce) almond
    paste or ½ teaspoon almond
    extract
1 teaspoon vanilla
½ teaspoon cinnamon

¼ teaspoon ground nutmeg
1 teaspoon butter
1 loaf (1 pound) day-old challah
    bread, cut into 1-inch cubes
⅓ cup dried cranberries
Carrot Crème Anglaise
    (recipe follows)

1. Heat oven to 350°F. Whisk cream and egg yolks together. Whisk in the next 5 ingredients (sugar through nutmeg) together until sugar and almond paste dissolve.

2. Spread the butter all over the bottom and sides of a 13 x 9 x 2 baking pan. Cover with bread cubes and sprinkle cranberries evenly on top.

3. Pour cream mixture over bread, making sure each cube is moistened. Soak at room temperature for about 10 minutes.

4. Set the pan into a larger pan in the oven and pour enough hot water into the larger pan to come half way up the sides of the

bread pan. Bake until a knife inserted in the center comes out almost clean, about 50 to 60 minutes. The center should jiggle just a little.

5. Cool slightly and serve with Carrot Crème Anglaise, or cool completely and refrigerate. Warm before serving.

NOTE: Be very careful about how much time the pudding spends at room temperature. Like other custards and mayonnaise, bread puddings are susceptible to bacteria that cause food illnesses, and should not be left out at room temperature for more than 2 hours, cumulative.

Carrot Crème Anglaise

I think this sauce would be a great accompaniment to a warm rice pudding or even a slice of yellow pound cake, but perhaps it's best over the preceding bread pudding recipe, which is a guest favorite at Bandon Dunes.

MAKES 3 CUPS

3 cups fresh carrot juice
2 cups heavy cream
1 teaspoon ground cardamom

1 teaspoon vanilla
9 egg yolks
1¾ cups sugar

1. Bring carrot juice to a boil in a saucepan over medium-high heat. Reduce until only ⅓ a cup is left, about 30 minutes. The mixture will smell like it's starting to caramelize and will create a lot of foam. Cool to room temperature.

2. Bring cream, cardamom, and vanilla just to a boil in a saucepan over medium-high heat. Remove from heat.

3. Whisk egg yolks with sugar and reduced carrot juice until smooth. Slowly drizzle a little of the hot cream mixture into the egg yolks, whisking constantly to prevent the eggs from cooking. Stir the warmed eggs back into the remaining hot cream mixture.

4. Place the saucepan over medium-low heat. Cook, stirring frequently, until the sauce is thickened, about 8 to 10 minutes. If you run your finger across the back of the spoon, the path your finger creates should stay clean. If the sauce runs through the path, it's not thick enough, and needs to cook a little longer. Do not allow sauce to boil. Remove from heat.

5. Strain sauce into a bowl then set that bowl in a larger bowl of ice water to chill, stirring occasionally while cooling. May be made 1 day in advance. Store covered in the refrigerator.

The Southwest

THE BOULDERS
RESORT AND GOLDEN DOOR SPA

P.O. Box 2090
Carefree, AZ 85377
800.553.1717
www.wyndam.com/luxury

Golf Courses:
North, South

Designer: Jay Morrish

Available holes: 36

Accommodations:
160 adobe casitas;
55 villas
(1, 2, or 3-bedroom)

Rates: $$–$$$$

Other Activities: Golden
Door Spa, tennis, rock-
climbing, hiking, shopping

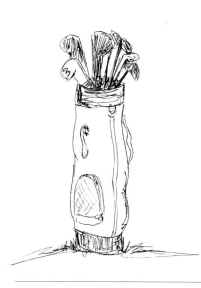

Sun-drenched adobe structures camouflaged among enormous granite rock clusters create an enchanting sense of place high in the Sonoran Desert northeast of Phoenix. Intimate and romantic might not be terms normally associated with golf resorts, but they do describe The Boulders Resort to a tee. For example, an optional "Tee Box" gourmet dinner marries romance with the beauty of the golf course, through music, lighted candles, champagne, and a table for two at sunset on the South course.

Women new to the game will appreciate the "Women to the Fore" program created to help heighten the learning curve and provide a relaxed, non-intimidating environment for novices. The program also provides equal access to tee times for all women golfers, regardless of skill.

Seven restaurants tempt guests with innovative regional and southwestern cuisine. The most formal, The Latilla (named after the massive hand-hewn logs and tree panels that create its circular ceiling) serves fresh, regionally influenced cuisine. The twinkling painted-desert ceiling in the Palo Verde sparks as much excitement as the exhibition kitchen where chefs prepare southwestern delicacies using a plethora of flavorful chiles and herbs. The Boulders Club, serving grilled steaks, chops, and seafood, offers spectacular golf course views.

A short walk through native desert leads to el Pedregal, an impressive adobe marketplace with shops, galleries, and two more Boulders restaurants, the festive Mexican-inspired Cantina and the quaint Bakery Café. Don't miss the chance to devour the Bakery's Saturday pork barbecue sandwich if given the opportunity.

All seven restaurants benefit from a forager on staff, whose job is to seek out local organic farmers and ranchers. Innovative spa cuisine appeared on the menus long before the addition of the world-renowned Golden Door Spa. The menus presented here are an exquisite example of healthful southwestern cuisine (well, everything except the worth-every-calorie dessert!)

Breakfast Menu

- CRUNCHY GRANOLA

- BLUE CORN PANCAKES

Dinner Menu

- SEARED SEA SCALLOPS
WITH WHITE BEANS & TOFU TARTAR SAUCE

- RED CHILE CHICKEN BREASTS
WITH BULGAR WHEAT & SWISS CHARD

- WARM BROWNIE SOUFFLÉ
WITH CINNAMON CHOCOLATE ICE CREAM

- *Recipe included*

Golf Pro's Tip

While playing desert golf, it is best to keep the golf ball out of the beautiful desert. If you tend to hit your ball off line, the first thing to check is your alignment. After you set up for a shot, place a club on the ground across your toes. Step back and place a second club down your target line (from where your ball lies) that is parallel to the first club. The second club should point in the direction of your target. If not, adjust your set up so that you're aiming correctly at the target. Good luck and hit it straight.

Signature Hole

South course, Number 5 — a narrow fairway leads to a dramatic rock outcropping sheltering the green on this long par 5. Desert views are unmatched, but don't get distracted. Precision is key.

Crunchy Granola

N ut-studded and mildly sweet, this granola is similar to the ones you might find in a whole foods grocery store in the bulk bin section, only it tastes significantly better because you make it fresh. My favorite dried fruits are blueberries and tart cherries.

MAKES 18 CUPS

1 cup flour
1 (18-ounce) container
   old-fashioned oats
1½ cups wheat germ
½ cup brown sugar
1 cup coconut
½ cup slivered almonds
½ cup cashew pieces

½ cup walnuts pieces
½ cup pistachios
½ cup chopped pecans
¼ cup hulled sunflower seeds
1 cup vegetable oil
1½ cups honey
2 cups dried fruit

1. Heat oven to 350°F. Stir the first 11 ingredients (flour through sunflower seeds) together.

2. Warm the oil and honey together in a saucepan over medium heat. Do not boil.

3. Pour honey mixture over oat mixture and stir to combine, until all the nuts and oats are coated.

4. Spray 2 large* baking sheets (with sides) with nonstick spray. Divide granola evenly between the 2 pans, spreading to edges. Bake until golden brown, about 20 minutes,

stirring every 7 to 10 minutes to promote even browning. (Rotate pans often if baking at the same time on separate racks, or bake 1 pan at a time.)

5. Remove from oven and stir in dried fruit. Stir occasionally while mixture is cooling to break up lumps. Store at room temperature in an airtight container for up to 1 month, or up to 3 months in the freezer.

I use a baking sheet that is 12 x 18 x 1. Any pan similar in size, even if a bit smaller, will work.

Blue Corn Pancakes

*T*he texture is similar to cornbread thanks to the blue corn meal, but it's not too grainy, like some recipes I've tried. Blueberries are a natural addition, so I added a handful of blueberries to each cake after ladling the batter into the skillet. They crush easily and streak the batter if you add them to the bowl instead of each individual pancake. I keep a container of dried buttermilk powder in my refrigerator (it's on the baking aisle) so that I can have these without having to have fresh buttermilk on hand. (See photograph on page P-6.)

MAKES 12 (4-INCH) PANCAKES

2 cups flour
½ cup blue corn meal
⅓ cup sugar
1½ teaspoons baking soda
¾ teaspoon baking powder

3 eggs
1½ cups buttermilk
2 tablespoons butter, melted
1½ cups fresh or frozen
　　blueberries (optional)

1. Stir the first 5 ingredients (flour through baking powder) together.

2. Beat the eggs with the buttermilk. Pour egg mixture over flour mixture and stir until just mixed. Stir in melted butter.

3. Heat a griddle or nonstick skillet over medium heat. Brush with butter or spray with nonstick spray. Ladle ¼ cup of batter for each pancake onto hot surface. (Sprinkle with a few blueberries if using.) Cook until edges start to dry and bubbles burst on surface, about 2 to 3 minutes.

4. Flip and cook on the other side until brown, about another minute or so. Keep warm in a 200°F oven until all the cakes are cooked. Serve with your favorite syrup.

B.Hillis

Seared Sea Scallops

WITH WHITE BEANS & TOFU TARTER SAUCE

*T*his is unbelievably good, amazingly quick to put together, and looks just beautiful on the plate. I'm beginning to think that there are some good spa cuisine chefs out there, after all. The key to nicely seared scallops is to pat them dry with a paper towel just before putting them into a hot skillet that has a thin film of oil or nonstick spray.

SERVES 4

12 sea scallops (about 1 pound)
Salt and freshly ground black pepper
1 cup vegetable broth
2 cups cooked white beans, drained
24 haricot verts (thin green beans), trimmed

¼ cup lemon juice
2 tablespoons chopped fresh parsley, divided
2 cups (about ½ small head) frisée lettuce, torn into small pieces
Tofu Tartar Sauce (recipe follows)

1. Heat oven to 250°F. Heat a nonstick skillet over medium-high heat. Pat scallops dry with paper towels, then season with salt and pepper. When pan is very hot, spray with nonstick spray. Add 6 scallops and sear until brown on one side, about 1½ minutes. Flip scallops over and sear the other side. Remove from pan and place on a baking sheet with sides in the oven to finish cooking while repeating with the remaining scallops, ensuring the pan returns to full heat before adding the next batch.

2. Pour the vegetable broth into the same skillet and bring to a simmer. Stir in the beans and simmer until liquid reduces by ⅓, about 5 to 6 minutes.

3. Stir in the haricot verts, lemon juice, and 1 tablespoon of parsley. Simmer 2 to 3 minutes, stirring occasionally. Turn off heat. Just before serving, stir in the frisée pieces, season with salt and pepper, and toss.

4. Divide the bean mixture between 4 warmed plates, using a slotted spoon, and saving the broth in the skillet. Mound the frisée and haricot verts to add height to the plate. Place 3 seared scallops around the bean and frisée mound.

5. Dot a teaspoon of tofu sauce (recipe follows) around the each scallop and drizzle the plates with remaining broth from the skillet.

Tofu Tartar Sauce:
5 ounces firm tofu, drained well and crumbled
4 teaspoons sweet pickle relish
¼ teaspoon dried dill (or ¾ teaspoon fresh)
Salt and freshly ground black pepper

1. Purée tofu in a small food processor. Stop and scrape the bowl a couple of times until the mixture is smooth. Remove to a small mixing bowl.

2. Stir in pickle relish, dill, and season with salt and pepper. Cover and chill until ready to use. May be prepared 2 days in advance.

Red Chile Chicken Breasts

WITH CURRIED YOGURT

*T*he sweet hot marinade reminds me of the thin barbecue sauces from the southeast, especially North Carolina, but this southwestern sauce has touches of other cultures, especially Asian (star anise and coriander) and Cajun (gumbo filé powder and allspice). Marinate the chicken overnight for the most flavorful results. It pairs perfectly with the bulgar wheat and Swiss chard side dish (see next recipe) the Boulders serves underneath the chicken. I won't mention that this is another healthy dish if you won't.

SERVES 4

4 (7-ounce) skinned, boned
    chicken breast halves

Marinade:
2 cups water
¼ cup mild pure ground chile
¼ cup brown sugar
¼ cup chopped cilantro leaves
¼ cup thinly sliced green onions

1½ teaspoons Mexican oregano*
2 star anise pods
1 teaspoon cayenne
¾ teaspoon ground coriander
¾ teaspoon filé powder (used in
    gumbo)
1 teaspoon chopped fresh mint
⅛ teaspoon ground allspice

1. Place all the marinade ingredients (water through allspice) in a saucepan over medium heat. Bring to a boil, stirring occasionally. Remove from heat and cool to room temperature. Reserve ½ cup.

2. Pour marinade over chicken breasts. Cover and marinate at least 4 hours or overnight in the refrigerator.

3. Heat oven to 350°F. Heat a nonstick ovenproof skillet over medium heat. Remove chicken from marinade. Season with salt. When pan is hot, sear chicken on both sides, about 2 minutes per side. Place skillet in oven and bake until chicken is done, about 14 to 16 minutes.

4. Reheat the reserved ½ cup marinade and drizzle over chicken breasts. Serve with Curried Yogurt (recipe follows).

Mexican oregano is not the same herb as the more common Mediterranean oregano. Look for Mexican oregano on the Mexican food aisle of your grocery store or see Sources, page 206, for ordering information.

Curried Yogurt:
1 cup plain low fat yogurt
2 tablespoons curry powder

Stir yogurt and curry powder until well blended. Cover and chill until ready to use.

Bulgar Wheat and Swiss Chard

*I*f all healthy dishes tasted this good, I'd eat healthy all the time. Bulgar wheat is not the same thing as cracked wheat, but it's close. Cracked wheat is just that, a whole wheat berry, cracked. Bulgar is the wheat berry with the outer bran removed, then steamed, dried, and cracked. I like the coarse grain, the kind they use to make the Middle Eastern salad, tabbouleh. Cook the bulgar wheat according to the directions on the package, but you may replace the water with vegetable broth to add more flavor.

SERVES 4

2 tablespoons thinly sliced
   green onion
1 tablespoon finely chopped
   red bell pepper
2 cups cooked bulgar wheat
   (about ¾ cup uncooked)

Salt and freshly ground black pepper
¼ cup vegetable broth
4 cups packed, cleaned, and stemmed
   Swiss chard (about ½ pound)

1. Heat a skillet over medium heat then spray with nonstick spray. Stir in the green onions and red bell pepper and cook about a minute. Stir in cooked bulgar and heat through. Season with salt and pepper. Keep warm.

2. Heat the vegetable broth in another skillet over medium heat and bring to a simmer. Add the Swiss chard and cook, turning with tongs, until chard is wilted and tender, about 5 minutes. Remove from skillet and pat dry with paper towels to remove excess moisture.

3. Divide the chard evenly among 4 warmed dinner plates. Top with ½ cup of bulgar wheat. (The resort then places sliced Red Chile Chicken on top and serves with Curried Yogurt.)

B. Hillis

Warm Brownie Soufflé
WITH CINNAMON CHOCOLATE ICE CREAM

Just when we were beginning to wonder if all recipes from the Boulders were going to be healthy, I unearthed this lovely little gem. Thank goodness! After all that nutritious stuff, we deserve a special treat. And, if that wasn't good enough, you can make these in advance and reheat before serving. Is that cool, or what?

SERVES 6

6 tablespoons butter
5¼ ounces chopped semisweet
   chocolate
⅔ cup sugar (plus more for dusting)
2 eggs
2 teaspoons bourbon

1½ teaspoons vanilla extract
⅔ cup flour
1½ teaspoons baking soda
6 chocolate truffles or
   chocolate kisses

1. Heat oven to 350°F. Heat butter in a saucepan until it comes to a boil. Remove from heat and add chocolate. Stir until chocolate is melted. Cool slightly.

2. Whip the ⅔ cup of sugar and eggs until stiff, about 5 minutes, using an electric mixer.

3. Pour melted chocolate mixture into whipped egg mixture and beat until incorporated.

4. Stir in the bourbon and vanilla.

5. Whisk the flour and baking soda together, and then fold evenly into the chocolate mixture. There should be no lumps.

6. Spray 6 (8-ounce) custard cups with nonstick spray and coat with sugar.

7. Ladle ⅓ cup batter (a #12 ice cream scoop is ⅓ cup) into each prepared cup.

Bake for 25 minutes, until batter has risen and top is crusty. Remove from oven.

8. If you are making these in advance, cool 15 to 20 minutes, and then remove from cups. Cool completely before wrapping tightly with plastic wrap to store in the refrigerator until ready to use. Unwrap soufflés, place on a baking sheet, and reheat in a preheated 350°F oven until warm throughout, about 5 to 8 minutes. Top with a truffle or kiss. Serve with a scoop of Cinnamon Chocolate Ice Cream (recipe follows).

9. If you want to serve right after baking, cool 15 minutes and remove from cups. Place on a baking sheet. Top each soufflé with a truffle or kiss and return to the oven for just a minute, not long enough to completely melt the candy. Serve with a scoop of Cinnamon Chocolate Ice Cream.

Cinnamon Chocolate Ice Cream

*H*ow easy could this be? You don't even have to make the ice cream yourself! I would seek out the delicate and citrusy cinnamon called Ceylon for this recipe. I order mine from Penzeys (see Sources, page 203). If you use the common cinnamon found on the grocery store shelf, cut back on the amount listed in the recipe by a teaspoon or it will be too strong.

MAKES 1 QUART

1 quart premium vanilla ice cream
1 tablespoon ground Ceylon
   cinnamon (see above)

4 ounces semisweet chocolate,
   melted

1. Refrigerate ice cream for 45 minutes or so to soften. Transfer to a large bowl and chop ice cream with a wooden spoon. Sprinkle with cinnamon and mix until cinnamon is well distributed. Drizzle in melted chocolate while stirring. The chocolate will begin to harden upon contact with the cold ice cream.

2. Transfer ice cream back into a container suitable for freezing. Cover and refreeze for 1 hour or more. May be prepared 3 days in advance.

CHILE OR CHILI?

I once had a debate with my editor (who also happens to be my dad) about how to spell "chile." He insisted that chile was supposed to end with an "i" not an "e." He reasoned that his favorite southwestern staple, a bowl of red chili, is spelled with an "i" and therefore the chile that went into the bowl of chili should be spelled the same way. (By the way, that bowl of red does not contain beans — we are Texans after all, and we don't put beans in chili.)

We tussled back and forth but finally agreed to let a third party settle the argument. I suggested we use *Webster's New World Dictionary of Culinary Arts* (Prentice Hall, 2nd Ed.) as the definitive source. Dad thought we should use *Webster's New World College Dictionary*. Not surprisingly, we each chose a source that supported our preferred spelling. According to the culinary dictionary, the word "chile" refers to the fruit of pepper plants belonging to the Capsicum family while "chili" refers to a stew-like dish prepared with chiles. The college dictionary defines "chile" simply as "chili." There you have it—the final answer. Either is correct. We did pick a preferred spelling for the pepper in this book — chile with an "e."

Chiles are commonly rated on a 1 to 10 heat scale, with 1 being the mildest and 10 being the hottest. The scale is based upon a test developed in 1912 by a pharmaceutical chemist named Wilbur Scoville. The Scoville test was somewhat subjective (asking people to taste as much pepper as they could stand). Today's tests are much more scientific and measure the actual level of capsaicin in each species. Capsaicin is the essential oil that causes the heat, found mostly in the seeds and membranes of peppers. Peppers on the same plant may vary in heat intensity. One jalapeño may rate a 5 on the heat scale, but another pepper from the same plant may rate an 8, or a 4. Remove the seeds and any white pithy membranes to tame a hot pepper. It's always a good idea to wear latex disposable kitchen gloves when handling fresh or dried chile peppers.

THE *Fairmont*
SCOTTSDALE PRINCESS

7575 East Princess Drive
Scottsdale, AZ 85255
480.585.4848
www.fairmont.com

Golf Courses:
TPC Stadium/Desert

Designer:
Tom Weiskopf and
Jay Morrish

Available holes: 36

Accommodations:
650 guest rooms,
including suites
and casitas

Rates: $–$$$$

Other Activities:
Willow Stream Spa,
tennis, Sonoran Splash
water park, shopping

Hazy purple mountains provide a stunning backdrop for this Spanish colonial-style resort. Dusk turns the desert rose-colored spread into an enchanting oasis. The long, tree-lined drive to the sparkling fountain at the entrance was made for stretch limousines. This Princess is the epitome of glamour.

Tiled open courtyards create a sense of spaciousness and covered walkways and doors that never seem to close blur the distinction between indoor and outdoor space. The Princess sees its fair share of celebrities as host to both golf and tennis championship tournaments in the mild warm winters.

In January, The PGA Tour stops at the resort's Tournament Players Club (TPC) Stadium Course. With galleries of more than 100,000, the Phoenix Open is one of the most popular stops on the tour, and the perfect chance for the Fairmont Scottsdale Princess to revel in the spotlight.

Phenomenal cuisine is one of many ways the resort shines. The culinary team makes a pilgrimage to foreign locations each year to broaden their knowledge and bring back new ideas to refresh the menus. The results are award-winning restaurants. Marquesa, AAA Five-Diamond restaurant, features the cuisine of the Mediterranean Riviera, blending Spanish, Italian and French influences. An open-air farmer's market-style brunch is a star on Sundays.

La Hacienda, the only Mobil Four-Star *and* AAA Four-Diamond gourmet Mexican restaurant in North America, is set in a free-standing 19th century Mexican ranch house and features authentic regional cuisine from all areas of Mexico. The Grill, overlooking the TPC Stadium course, is for serious steak and seafood aficionados. A few favorite recipes from The Grill are presented here. It's easy to take home some of the flavors of the Scottsdale Princess — the chefs have created *Flavors,* a line of specialty foods available for sale, such as Mango Habañero Hot Sauce, Garlic Queso, and Prickly Pear Syrup.

Breakfast Menu

- OATMEAL BRÛLÉE

- PRIME STEAK HASH WITH
- MUSHROOM COUNTRY GRAVY
  OVER BUTTERMILK BISCUITS

- PRINCESS PUZZLE BREAD

Dinner Menu

- ROCK SHRIMP STRUDEL WITH SUN-DRIED
  YELLOW TOMATO SAUCE

PANCETTA-WRAPPED MONKFISH WITH YELLOW TOMATO FONDUE

- TRUFFLE MASHED POTATOES

- CARAMEL APPLE TARTS WITH
- STICKY BUN ICE CREAM

- *Recipe included*

Golf Pro's Tip

In windy conditions, most golfers panic. With the right approach and club selection, you can master the wind. When playing into a gusty wind, select one or two clubs up from what you would normally choose with no wind. Choke down on the club to give you more control. Play the ball toward the back of your stance and swing smoothly.

Signature Hole

TPC Stadium Course, Number 15 — a reachable par 5 with water surrounding an island green. Bunkers flanking both sides of the green add an additional challenge.

Oatmeal Brûlée

*M*ore dessert-like with the addition of a custard layer than the one served at the Sagamore (see page 198), I found my tasters licking the ramekins clean, and one asked if she could take another one to go. Use 8-ounce custard cups or ramekins, which are large enough to hold ¾-cup of cooked oatmeal and a thin layer of custard and brown sugar. The custard may be made the day before, and use any leftover custard as a dessert sauce within the next day or two.

Vanilla Custard:
(Makes 2 cups)

½ vanilla bean, split
   (or ½ teaspoon vanilla extract)
¾ cup milk
¾ cup heavy cream
1 cup sugar, divided
5 egg yolks, lightly beaten

To make custard:

1. Scrape the vanilla bean seeds into a saucepan with the milk, cream, and ½ cup sugar. (Save the vanilla bean to flavor sugar or discard.) Stir the milk mixture and bring just to a boil over medium heat, stirring occasionally.

2. Whisk the remaining ½ cup of sugar with the beaten egg yolks. Slowly drizzle a little of the hot milk mixture into the egg yolks, whisking constantly to prevent the eggs from cooking. Stir the warmed eggs back into the remaining hot milk mixture.

3. Place the saucepan over medium-low heat. Cook, stirring frequently, until the sauce thickens, about 8 to 10 minutes. Do not allow sauce to boil. If you run your finger across the back of the spoon, the path your finger creates should stay clean. If the sauce runs through the path, it's not thick enough and needs to cook a little longer.

4. Strain sauce into a bowl then set that bowl in a larger bowl of ice water to chill, stirring occasionally while cooling. May be made 1 day in advance. Store covered in the refrigerator.

For each serving:

¾ cup cooked oatmeal
2 tablespoons vanilla custard
1 tablespoon brown sugar
2 tablespoons fresh berries
   (optional garnish)
Mint (optional garnish)

To assemble Brûlée:

1. Heat broiler to high (see note). Place cooked oatmeal in an 8-ounce ovenproof custard cup.

2. Spoon 2 tablespoons vanilla custard evenly over top.

3. Sprinkle brown sugar evenly over custard. (Don't worry if the sugar sinks into the custard.)

4. Place custard cups on a baking sheet and place under broiler (about 3-inches from heat) and brown top about 1 to 3 minutes, depending upon the heat of your broiler. Watch carefully! Remove from heat. Using oven mitts, place hot cup onto serving plate.

5. Garnish with fresh berries and mint (optional).

NOTE: Alternatively, use a kitchen torch to brown the top. The advantage of a kitchen torch is that it doesn't heat the ramekin as much, but the disadvantage is that it takes longer to brown than the broiler.

Prime Steak Hash

*H*ere's a terrific way to use leftover steak. The resort splits a large buttermilk biscuit in half, places a scoop of this hash on one biscuit half, and pours a special country gravy over the other half. Just to take it completely over the top, perched on each biscuit half is a perfectly poached egg. Most excellent!

SERVES 6

1 tablespoon olive oil
¼ cup chopped onion
¼ cup chopped red bell pepper
¼ cup chopped green bell pepper
2 tablespoons peeled and
    chopped carrot
2 tablespoons chopped celery
1 tablespoon minced garlic
3 tablespoons butter, divided
1 portabella mushroom cap, chopped

1 cup (2 ounces) sliced button
    mushrooms
1½ pounds russet potatoes, baked,
    cooled, peeled, and chopped
    (3 cups)
8 ounces cooked beef tenderloin or
    strip loin pieces
2 tablespoons chopped fresh herbs
    (parsley, basil, thyme, etc.)
Salt and freshly ground black pepper

1. Heat olive oil in a large skillet over medium-high heat. Cook onions, red and green peppers, carrot, celery, and garlic for a minute or so, until fragrant.

2. Add 1 tablespoon of butter to skillet and stir in portabella and button mushrooms. Cook for about 2 minutes, until mushrooms begin to soften.

3. Add the remaining 2 tablespoons of butter and stir in potatoes. Cook, flipping the bottom to the top once or twice, until the potatoes brown, about 5 to 8 minutes.

4. Stir in the beef and heat through, another 2 minutes. Stir in the herbs. Taste and season with salt and pepper.

Mushroom Country Gravy

T he herbs make this gravy far superior to the average breakfast gravy. Treat yourself to the full-blown resort version, with fluffy buttermilk biscuits on the bottom, Prime Steak Hash (previous recipe) on top of one biscuit half with this gravy smothering the other half. It's worth the splurge. Of course, this gravy is perfectly capable of standing on its own over any biscuit or piece of toast. Chef Cathy Rosenberg, who graciously proofread this book, made a note in the margin that this gravy would be fabulous over a baked potato, too.

MAKES 3 CUPS

8 ounces pork sausage
1 cup chopped onion
1 tablespoon minced garlic
2 cups (4 ounces) sliced
   button mushrooms
½ cup flour
2 cups milk

2 tablespoons thinly sliced green
   onions
1 tablespoon chopped fresh
   basil leaves
1 tablespoon fresh thyme leaves
1 tablespoon chopped fresh parsley
Salt and freshly ground black pepper

1. Brown sausage in a large skillet over medium heat until completely cooked, about 8 to 10 minutes. Place sausage in a strainer to drain. Wipe out skillet with a paper towel and return drained sausage to skillet over medium heat. Stir in onions, and cook until softened, about 2 minutes.

2. Stir in garlic and mushrooms, cooking until mushrooms are tender, about 4 to 5 minutes.

3. Sprinkle with flour and stir until flour is absorbed. Cook another 2 minutes, stirring

occasionally, to release the starch in the flour. Pour in 2 cups of milk and stir constantly for a minute or so, while the mixture thickens.

4. Stir in green onions and herbs, cooking until the mixture is thick. Taste and season with salt and pepper. May be made 1 day in advance. Cool completely then cover and store in the refrigerator. Gently reheat before serving, adding a little milk to thin if necessary.

Princess Puzzle Bread

*M*onkey Bread is a sweet yeast dough rolled into clumps, dipped in butter, and baked together so that the pieces join to form one loaf. This is the Princess Resort's version, with much smaller clumps of dough and far too good to be left alone in a room with me. Tempting raspberry and honey coated dough pieces baked to golden brown that pull apart easily, too easily, means everyone should gather 'round as soon as it comes out of the oven. You could make this in individual muffin tins, as the resort does, or in one pan as I did. Start this the night before because the dough needs to rise overnight in the refrigerator.

SERVES 6

Dough:
½ cup warm (not hot) milk
2¼ teaspoons (.25 ounce) dry yeast
1 cup flour (first addition)
8 tablespoons (1 stick) butter,
    softened
½ cup sugar
Pinch salt
2 eggs
1 cup flour (second addition)

Filling:
1 cup brown sugar
8 tablespoons (1 stick) butter,
    softened
3 tablespoons of honey
1 teaspoon vanilla extract

½ cup raspberry jam
1 teaspoon cinnamon

To make the dough:

1. Whisk the milk and yeast together in a large bowl until the yeast dissolves. Stir in 1 cup of flour. Cover with a towel and set aside until mixture ferments and doubles in size, about an hour in a warm kitchen, a little longer if your kitchen is not warm.

2. Beat the butter, sugar, and salt with an electric mixer (use the paddle attachment if you are using a stand mixer). Beat in the eggs until smooth. Beat in the fermented dough. Mix until well blended.

3. Switch to the dough hook attachment and mix in the last cup of flour. Mix on slow speed for about 5 minutes to develop the dough. It will be a loose, sticky dough. Place in a lightly oiled large bowl. Cover bowl with plastic wrap and refrigerate overnight.

4. To make the sugar filling, beat the brown sugar and butter together until fluffy, about 1 minute with an electric mixer. Drizzle in the honey and vanilla, beating until smooth. Divide the sugar mixture in half.

5. Spread half the sugar filling over the bottom and sides of a 10-inch deep-dish pie pan or other similar pan with sides at least 2-inches high.

6. To the other half of the sugar, mix in the raspberry jam and cinnamon.

7. Remove the dough from the refrigerator and cut into 1½-inch cubes. Toss the cubes with the raspberry-sugar mixture until well coated.

8. Place the coated cubes in the prepared pan, with the cubes snugly touching each other.

continued on next page

9. Cover lightly with plastic wrap, then a kitchen towel and set in a warm spot free from drafts until it almost doubles in size, about 1 hour or so.

10. Heat oven to 350° F. Bake puzzle bread for 30 to 40 minutes, or until medium brown in the center and darker brown on the edges. Don't use your bare finger to see if the bread bounces back to the touch (which it will when done) because the sugar coating will burn your finger. Use a towel to protect your finger if you test this way.

11. Remove from oven and immediately (and carefully with mitts) invert bread onto a serving plate. Shake the baking dish if necessary to release the bread. Cool a few minutes then serve warm.

Rock Shrimp Strudel
WITH SUN-DRIED YELLOW TOMATO SAUCE

*T*his is really quite elegant, with a delicately crisp phyllo shell, a zingy filling, and a sweet, tart sauce. Rock shrimp (named for its rock hard shell) is usually peeled and frozen, with anywhere from 70 to 90 pieces per pound. The flavor is sweet, similar to lobster. Substitute another similar size shrimp if you can't find rock shrimp. (See photograph on page P-7.)

SERVES 6 TO 8

4 tablespoons butter
$\frac{1}{4}$ cup flour + 2 tablespoons
2 tablespoons vegetable oil
1 cup chopped onion
1 cup chopped green bell pepper
$\frac{1}{2}$ cup chopped fennel bulb
1 tablespoon minced garlic
1 pound rock shrimp, peeled
    and deveined

2 Roma tomatoes, seeded
    and chopped
$\frac{1}{2}$ cup white wine
$\frac{1}{4}$ cup water
Salt and freshly ground black pepper
10 sheets phyllo dough
8 tablespoons (1 stick) butter, melted
Sun-Dried Yellow Tomato Sauce
    (recipe follows)

1. Make a roux by melting 4 tablespoons of butter in a small skillet over medium heat. Whisk in flour and cook until mixture smells nutty and turns a slight shade of golden brown, about 4 to 5 minutes. Set roux aside.

2. Heat vegetable oil in a large skillet over medium-high heat. Stir in onions, bell pepper, fennel, and garlic. Cook until onions are soft, about 3 to 4 minutes.

3. Mix in shrimp and tomatoes. Cook until tomatoes are soft and shrimp are almost, but not quite done, about 2 minutes, stirring frequently. Stir in white wine and water.

4. Stir in warm roux, and simmer until mixture thickens, about a minute. Remove from heat and season with salt and pepper. Cool. May be prepared 1 day in advance. Cool completely. Cover and store in the refrigerator.

5. Heat oven to 400°F. Unwrap phyllo dough and keep covered.

6. Remove 1 sheet and place on a work surface. Brush liberally with melted butter. Top with another sheet, keeping the rest covered. Butter 2nd sheet. Top with a 3rd

sheet and butter. Repeat until you have 5 buttered sheets.

7. Turn buttered phyllo sheets so that a long side is closest to you. Spread $\frac{1}{2}$ of the cooled shrimp mixture between the center of the stacked sheets and the edge facing you, leaving a 3-inch border on the bottom and sides. Starting at the bottom, roll the phyllo dough over the filling. After one roll, fold in the sides; then continue rolling to create a log about 17 inches long, 3 inches wide and 2 inches tall.

8. Repeat steps 6 and 7 with the remaining 5 phyllo sheets and remaining filling.

9. Place the logs on a baking sheet with sides, lined with parchment paper or a silicone mat. Butter generously with more melted butter. Cut 5 slits at an angle on the top of each log to allow steam to escape while baking.

10. Place in the preheated oven and bake until golden brown, about 18 to 22 minutes. Remove and cool 10 minutes before slicing. Serve with Sun-Dried Yellow Tomato Sauce (recipe follows).

Sun-Dried Yellow Tomato Sauce

*S*weet and tangy, this light sauce complements the richness of the shrimp strudel, and may be made a couple of days in advance. It's also a lovely sauce for grilled fish, especially halibut. The resort uses yellow sun-dried tomatoes. If you can't find them, substitute regular red sun-dried ones, but not the kind packed in oil.

MAKES 2 TO 2½ CUPS

1 cup (3 ounces) sun-dried
   yellow tomatoes
2 cups hot chicken or vegetable stock
¼ cup red wine vinegar

¼ cup sugar
1 teaspoon minced garlic
Salt and freshly ground
   black pepper

1. Soak tomatoes in hot stock until soft, about 20 minutes. Drain tomatoes, reserving liquid.

2. Place tomatoes, vinegar, sugar, and garlic in a blender. Add enough liquid to purée mixture to an applesauce consistency. You might use all of the liquid or have just a little left over.

3. Strain sauce and season with salt and pepper. Reheat if necessary before serving with the Rock Shrimp Strudel (previous recipe). May be made 2 days in advance. Chill, covered. Reheat before serving.

Truffle Mashed Potatoes

*I*ndulging in pure opulence, the resort garnishes these already luscious potatoes with chunks of poached lobster meat and serves them as a base for Pancetta-Wrapped Monkfish. Try them with your next grilled steak or chop.

SERVES 4 TO 6

2½ pounds Yukon gold or russet
   potatoes, peeled, and cut into
   2-inch cubes
4 tablespoons (½ stick) butter
½ cup heavy cream

2 teaspoons white truffle oil*
1 tablespoon finely chopped
   fresh chives
Salt and freshly ground
   white pepper

1. Boil potatoes in salted water until tender, about 20 to 25 minutes. Drain.

2. Heat butter and cream in a small saucepan over medium heat. Do not boil.

3. Mash potatoes with warm butter and cream mixture. Stir in more warm cream if

you prefer a thinner potato mash. Stir in truffle oil, chives, and season with salt and white pepper. Serve warm.

*Truffle oil is available in fine kitchen stores, gourmet shops, specialty grocery stores, and through the Internet. See Sources, page 203.

Caramel Apple Tarts

*D*arling individual pies filled with tart apples, gooey caramel sauce, and a sweet crunchy topping make this a fabulous choice when you need that extra splash. Start the filling at least the night before, but by completing all the components a day or two in advance, it won't seem like a chore to assemble and bake this all-American dessert, and you'll be a hero. I think each tart easily feeds two after a multi-course meal. The resort uses special oval molds, about 2-inches tall. I've chosen the widely available miniature tart pans with a removable bottom, available at most kitchen stores.

MAKES 6 (4½-INCH) MINIATURE TARTS

Apple filling:
8 small Granny Smith apples
   (3¼ pounds)
3 tablespoons butter
½ cup sugar
½ vanilla bean, split
1 stick cinnamon (or pinch of
   ground cinnamon)

Caramel sauce:
2 cups sugar
¾ cup water
2 cups heavy cream
4 tablespoons butter

Sugar dough:
¾ cup (1½ sticks) butter
½ cup sugar
1 egg
⅛ teaspoon vanilla extract
1½ cups flour
1½ teaspoons baking powder
Flour for dusting

Streusel topping:
½ cup (1 stick) butter, slightly
   softened
½ cup brown sugar
⅛ teaspoon cinnamon
2 cups cake flour

To make filling:

1. Peel, core, and cut the apples into ½-inch slices. Melt the butter in a very large, deep skillet over medium-high heat. Stir in the sugar, vanilla bean, and cinnamon stick. Cook until the butter browns slightly, about 3 minutes.

2. Mix in the apples (pan will be very full — divide between two pans to cook if necessary) and simmer, stirring frequently, until apples are soft but still hold their shape, about 10 minutes. Remove from heat and drain off any excess moisture. Cool, then cover and chill overnight.

To make the caramel sauce:

1. Stir the sugar and water together in a tall saucepan over medium heat. Stop stirring

and let the mixture come to a boil. Swirl the pan as the sugar turns golden brown to distribute the color. When dark golden brown, remove from heat. The whole caramel process takes anywhere from 15 to 25 minutes.

2. Slowly and carefully pour in the cream, a little at a time. The mixture will bubble up violently so keep your hands out of the way.

3. Stir in the butter and return the mixture to medium heat to dissolve any clumps that formed when the cream was added. Stir until smooth. Remove from heat and cool completely. Cover and chill until needed. The sauce will be mixed with the apples later.

continued on next page

To make the dough:

1. Beat the butter and sugar until fluffy, about 2 minutes. Beat in the egg and vanilla.

2. Stir in the flour and baking powder just until the dough comes together. Wrap in plastic wrap and chill for at least 2 hours or overnight.

To make streusel topping:

Rub all ingredients together until crumbly and there are no large lumps of butter. The mixture will resemble coarse meal.

Putting it all together:

1. Remove chilled dough from refrigerator and divide into 6 equal pieces, about 2½ ounces each. Flour your hands.

2. Pat each piece of dough into a circle and place in a 4½-inch tart pan with a removable bottom. Pat the dough gently, working it over the bottom and up the sides of the tart pan to cover evenly.

3. Trim any excess from top of tart pan. Be careful not to overwork the dough. You'll be good at this by the time you do the sixth tart. Refrigerate tart shells for at least 30 minutes. Wrap with plastic wrap if chilling for more than 30 minutes.

4. Meanwhile, heat oven to 350°F. Remove vanilla bean and cinnamon stick from apple filling. Stir in ½ cup of caramel sauce, reserving the remaining caramel sauce.

5. Place tart pans on a lined baking sheet. Fill each pan to the top with apple filling, about a generous ½ cup. Cover completely with streusel mixture, about ⅓ a cup per tart, mounding slightly.

6. Bake for 35 to 40 minutes or until golden brown. Remove from oven and let cool 10 to 15 minutes. Remove from tart pan and place on a dessert plate.

7. Serve with remaining caramel sauce and a scoop of Sticky Bun Ice Cream (recipe follows).

Sticky Bun Ice Cream

*W*hoa! Caramel and pecans swirled in rich, creamy, homemade vanilla ice cream? Sounds too good to be true but it is true and it is really, really good. Save some for the apple tarts.

Makes 1 quart

½ cup pecan halves
½ cup caramel sauce
¼ cup honey
½ teaspoon cinnamon
½ vanilla bean, split (or ½ teaspoon vanilla extract)

2 cups milk
2 cups heavy cream
1 cup sugar, divided
8 egg yolks

1. Heat oven to 350°F. Stir pecan halves, caramel sauce, honey, and cinnamon together in a small baking dish. Bake for 10 minutes, stirring occasionally, until mixture is hot and bubbly. Remove from oven and cool.

2. Scrape the vanilla bean seeds into a saucepan with the milk, heavy cream, and ½ cup sugar. (Save the vanilla bean to flavor sugar or discard.) Turn heat to medium and bring mixture just to a boil, stirring occasionally. Remove from heat and let steep for 10 minutes.

3. Whisk the remaining ½ cup of sugar with the egg yolks. Slowly drizzle a little of the hot cream mixture into the egg mixture,

whisking constantly to prevent the eggs from cooking. Stir the warmed eggs back into the remaining hot cream mixture.

4. Place the saucepan over medium heat and cook until the mixture thickens, about 5 to 8 minutes. Strain into a bowl, then set that bowl in a larger bowl of ice water to chill, stirring occasionally, until mixture is cold to the touch.

5. Process in an ice cream maker according to manufacturer's directions. Fold in pecan mixture and transfer to a suitable container for freezing. Freeze for at least 8 hours or overnight.

VENTANA CANYON

6200 North
Clubhouse Lane
Tucson, AZ 85750
800.828.5701
www.wyndham.com/luxury

Golf Courses: Ventana
Canyon Golf & Racquet
Club: Mountain/ Canyon

Designer: Tom Fazio

Available holes: 36

Accommodations:
50 suites

Rates: $–$$$$

Other Activities: Spa,
fitness center, tennis, hiking

With only 50 spacious but cozy suites, The Lodge at Ventana Canyon is the most intimate resort in Par Fork! Painted desert skies, sweeping vistas of saguaro and prickly pear are daily companions to this tiny resort at the base of the 9,000-foot Santa Catalina Mountains in northeastern Tucson. There are nearly as many golf holes as there are guestrooms, all sculpted by the master architect, Tom Fazio.

Both courses offer challenging play. The terrain directly impacts the Mountain course, with some steep climbs to tee boxes. The desert is a force to be reckoned with on every hole on both courses. As with many desert courses, water comes into play only on a few holes, most critically on the Canyon number 18 where a pond hugs the back and side of the green. Few courses offer such striking natural scenery.

The golf course isn't the only place where one may marvel at the unfettered beauty of the high Sonoran Desert, or catch a glimpse of the native wildlife that includes quail, coyotes, and an occasional bobcat. The Hearthstone dining room offers floor-to-ceiling windows for more panoramic beauty while providing innovative regional Southwestern cuisine with impeccable service. More than 300 days of sunshine coupled with moderate temperatures most of the year means outdoor dining is often the preferred choice among guests.

Breakfast Menu

- ZUCCHINI MUFFINS

- RANCHERO-STYLE EGGS WITH SALSA FRESCA

- SOUTHWESTERN COUNTRY POTATOES

Dinner Menu

- GRILLED SALMON WITH SCALLION CAPER BEURRE BLANC

- ASPARAGUS, MUSHROOM & SPINACH SAUTÉ

- BLACK & WHITE NAPOLEONS WITH FRESH BERRIES

- *Recipe included*

Golf Pro's Tip

Tom Fazio created a challenging layout at Ventana Canyon with mult-tiered greens. The key to good scoring on each hole is to know on what tier the hole is cut before playing your shot to the green, and trying to place it on that tier. Always play each shot as if it were the first shot of the day.

Signature Hole

Mountain course, Number 3 — plays across 107 yards of cactus and canyons, offering desert wilderness views that stretch for miles south across the Sonoran Desert.

Zucchini Muffins

*T*hese taste almost like cookies, they're very sweet and especially crunchy if you make miniature muffins instead of standard muffins. Don't bake miniature muffins quite as long. Start checking after 12 minutes of baking for the little guys.

MAKES 24 STANDARD MUFFINS

4½ cups flour
2¼ cups sugar
1½ teaspoons baking powder
1½ teaspoons baking soda
½ teaspoon salt
1½ teaspoons cinnamon
5 eggs

1½ cups oil
4 teaspoons vanilla extract
2¼ cups grated zucchini
   (about 8 ounces)
1½ cups raisins
1½ cups walnuts

1. Heat oven to 350°F. Spray 2 (12-count) muffin pans with nonstick spray.

2. Whisk the first 6 ingredients (flour through cinnamon) together in a large bowl.

3. Beat the eggs with the oil and vanilla extract. Stir in the zucchini.

4. Pour the egg mixture over the flour mixture and mix just until barely moistened,

folding in raisins and walnuts at the end. Do not overmix. Small lumps are fine.

5. Scoop ¼ cup portions into each muffin tin (a #20 ice cream scoop works great).

6. Bake until a toothpick inserted in the center comes out clean, about 15 to 18 minutes.

Ranchero-Style Eggs

$\mathcal{T}$he chef doesn't like for you to go hungry after breakfast at the Lodge. You might have to wrestle a mountain lion in the foothills of the Santa Catalinas, so he sends you out with copious chow to keep up your strength. I'm kidding — at least about the mountain lion part, not about the portion size. This is one of my all-time favorite southwestern breakfasts. Make the Ranchero Sauce and salsa the day before and then this is a snap to put together.

SERVES 4 TO 8

8 corn tortillas
4 teaspoons vegetable oil
8 eggs, cooked any way
8 thin slices (7 ounces) Monterey Jack
    cheese with peppers
2 cups Ranchero Sauce, warmed
    (recipe follows)
2 cups Salsa Fresca (recipe follows)
1 large avocado

1. Heat oven to 350°F. Lightly brush tortillas with vegetable oil, place on a baking sheet, and bake until crisp, about 10 minutes, turning half way through baking. Remove from oven and place 2 tortillas per person on ovenproof plates, overlapping slightly. Increase oven temperature to 400°F.

2. Top tortillas with 2 cooked eggs (scrambled, fried, or poached), $\frac{1}{2}$ cup of Ranchero sauce (recipe follows) and 2 slices of cheese. Return plates to oven to melt cheese, about 2 to 3 minutes.

3. Cut avocado in half and remove seed. Peel avocado and cut each half into slices, about $\frac{1}{4}$-inch thick.

4. Remove plates from oven and fan avocado slices on top of each plate. Place a scoop of Salsa Fresca (recipe follows) on the side.

Ranchero Sauce (Makes 3 cups)
1 tablespoon vegetable oil
2 cups chopped onion
$1\frac{1}{2}$ cups chopped green bell pepper
2 teaspoons minced garlic
$1\frac{1}{4}$ pounds tomatoes, seeded and
    chopped (about 3 cups)
1 cup tomato juice
$1\frac{1}{2}$ teaspoons ground cumin
$1\frac{1}{2}$ teaspoons chile powder
$1\frac{1}{2}$ teaspoons ground Mexican oregano*
$1\frac{1}{2}$ teaspoons lemon juice
Salt and freshly ground black pepper

1. Heat oil in a saucepan over medium heat. Stir in onions, bell pepper, and garlic. Cook until onions are soft, about 4 to 5 minutes, stirring occasionally.

2. Mix in tomatoes, juice, spices, and lemon juice, and bring to a boil. Reduce heat and simmer for 30 minutes, stirring occasionally. Season with salt and pepper. May be prepared up to 2 days in advance. Store covered in the refrigerator. Reheat gently before serving.

*Mexican oregano is not the same herb as the more common Mediterranean oregano. Look for Mexican oregano on the Mexican food aisle of your grocery store or see Sources, page 206, for ordering information.

continued on next page

Salsa Fresca (Makes 3 cups)

Leave the jalapeño seeds in if you like some heat like I do.

1 pound ripe tomatoes, seeded
   and chopped
½ cup chopped onion
½ cup chopped green bell pepper
1½ teaspoons minced garlic
½ jalapeño, seeded and minced
¼ cup tomato juice
1 tablespoon lime juice
2 teaspoons olive oil
¼ cup chopped fresh cilantro
Salt and freshly ground black pepper

Mix all ingredients together and season to taste with salt and pepper. May be prepared 1 day in advance. Store covered in the refrigerator. Bring to room temperature before serving.

Southwestern Country Potatoes

*S*imple and flavorful as written, I also like to add a kick by sprinkling the potatoes with a little pure ground chile or hot chile powder before they finish browning.

SERVES 4 TO 6

2 pounds small red potatoes
1 tablespoon olive oil
1 tablespoon butter
¼ cup chopped red onion

¼ cup chopped green bell pepper
1 tablespoon minced garlic
1 tablespoon chopped fresh cilantro
Salt and freshly ground black pepper

1. Cut potatoes into quarters, and steam until almost done, about 10 to 12 minutes. Spread on a baking sheet to dry.

2. Heat olive oil and butter in a large skillet over medium heat. When hot, add partially cooked potatoes and onions, and cook until

potatoes begin to brown, stirring once or twice, about 8 to 10 minutes.

3. Stir in bell peppers, garlic, and cilantro and cook until bell peppers soften, another 2 to 3 minutes. Season with salt and pepper.

B.Hillis

Grilled Salmon

WITH A SCALLION CAPER BEURRE BLANC

I love salmon but I'm not big on the smell of cooking it in the house, so outdoor grilling is the perfect solution. The recipe calls for the skin on, because it protects the fish better on the grill. You can still do this with skinless salmon, just oil your grill really well and shave about a minute off the grilling time. The chef serves this dish with jasmine rice and a vegetable sauté of asparagus, exotic mushrooms, and baby spinach. Beurre blanc is a traditional French butter sauce, and this one is mildly flavored with green onions and salty capers.

SERVES 4

4 (6 to 8-ounce) salmon fillets, skin on
¼ cup olive oil
Salt and freshly ground black pepper
1½ cups Scallion Beurre Blanc
   (recipe follows)

1. Heat the grill to medium-high (375° to 400°F). Brush both sides of the salmon with the olive oil, and season with salt and pepper.

2. Grill skin side up for 4 minutes, flip and grill until medium temperature, roughly another 4 minutes, depending upon how thick the salmon is. Cook another minute or so for medium-well or well done.

3. Remove skin before serving. Serve with Scallion Beurre Blanc (recipe follows).

Scallion Beurre Blanc (Makes 1½ cups)

Adding a splash of cream at the end helps stabilize this delicate butter sauce.

1 cup dry white wine
2 tablespoons capers, drained
2 tablespoons chopped green onions
   (green and white part)
8 tablespoons (1 stick) cold butter,
   cut into cubes
Splash of heavy cream (optional)
Salt and freshly ground white pepper

1. Heat white wine, capers, and green onions in a saucepan over medium-high heat. Reduce until only 2 to 3 tablespoons of liquid remain, about 12 to 15 minutes. Turn heat to low and remove pan from heat.

2. Whisk in cold butter, a few cubes at a time. Place the pan back on the fire to keep sauce warm (but don't leave it there long), constantly whisking. Continue to add a little butter at a time, whisking until all the butter is used. If the sauce starts to look oily (the butter is separating), then add the splash of cream and whisk over low heat for a few seconds.

3. Season with salt and white pepper. Serve immediately.

Asparagus, Mushroom, & Spinach Sauté

Once called wild mushrooms, exotic varieties like shiitake, oyster, cremini (and its larger form, portabella) found in most grocery stores today are actually cultivated on mushroom farms, not found in the wild. You should always be wary of mushrooms picked from or found in the wild forests, eating only those picked by professional foragers.

SERVES 4

1 teaspoon butter
1 teaspoon olive oil
4 cups sliced exotic mushrooms
   (no stems)
1 teaspoon minced shallots

½ teaspoon minced garlic
1 pound asparagus, trimmed
8 cups (5 ounces) fresh baby spinach
Salt and freshly ground black pepper

1. Heat the butter and olive oil in a large skillet over medium-high heat.

2. Add the mushrooms, shallots, and garlic. Cook, stirring occasionally for a minute or two.

3. Cut the asparagus into 2-inch pieces, at an angle. Stir the asparagus into the mushroom mixture. Cook for a minute or so.

4. Add baby spinach to the skillet and cook, turning and stirring the mixture until the spinach is wilted, about 2 to 3 minutes.

5. Cover and let rest for 2 to 3 minutes. Season with salt and pepper.

Black & White Napoleons

WITH FRESH BERRIES

....

*T*his is a "WOW" dessert, worth every minute it takes to make the components and assemble it. My friends Candy and Quentin weren't quite sure whether to take a picture of it or eat it — so we did both. Napoleons are traditionally made with puff pastry dough layered with pastry cream, but lately, pastry chefs are calling anything layered and stacked a "Napoleon." I think he would have approved of this one. (See photograph on page P-8.)

SERVES 8

24 black cookies (recipe follows)
2 cups vanilla cream (recipe follows)
2 cups mixed fresh berries
  (blueberries, raspberries,
  blackberries, sliced strawberries)

Garnish:
8 fresh whole strawberries
Powdered sugar
8 mint sprigs

1. Lay 8 black cookie rounds on a sheet pan. Spread a tablespoon of vanilla cream on top, covering cookie. Place a handful of berries on top of the cream, and spread a thin layer of cream on top of the berries.

2. Place another cookie round on top, press very gently, and repeat with cream, berries, cream, with a final cookie round on top. You'll have 3 layers of cookie and 2 layers of cream and berries.

3. Garnish with a sprinkle of powdered sugar, a fresh strawberry on top, and a sprig of mint.

Black Cookie Layer:
(Makes 24 3-inch cookies)

2 (1-pound) packages of Oreo® cookies
2¼ cups chopped pecans
½ cup toasted coconut*
1 cup (2 sticks) butter, melted

1. Heat oven to 350°F. Pulse cookies in 2 batches in a food processor until finely ground. Grind pecans and toasted coconut in a food processor until finely ground.

2. Toss ground cookies, pecans, and coconut together in a large bowl. Pour melted butter all over mixture and toss until well mixed.

3. Divided mixture between 2 jellyroll pans (15 x 10 x 1). Press cookie crumb mixture into the pan. Take your time doing this so that it's even and firm. Filling should be ½-inch thick.

4. Bake for 10 minutes. Remove and let cool completely.

5. Cut 12 (3-inch) circles with a sharp cookie cutter from each pan. Don't remove any of the circles until you cut all 12. These cookies are very delicate and will break if handled roughly. I found it was a little easier to cut if the cookies were slightly chilled, but not too cold. Freeze leftover cookie crumbs to use as the crust for your next cheesecake.

*To toast coconut, see page 18, under Common Procedures.

continued on next page

Vanilla Cream:
(Makes 2 cups)
⅔ cup sugar
⅓ cup corn starch
¼ teaspoon salt
2 cups half-and-half
2 egg yolks
1 teaspoon vanilla extract
½ vanilla bean, split

1. Whisk sugar, cornstarch, and salt together in a saucepan. Whisk in half-and-half, yolks, and vanilla extract. Scrape vanilla bean seeds into mixture with a sharp knife. (Save vanilla bean to flavor sugar or discard.)

2. Place mixture over medium heat. Bring to a boil, stirring occasionally, about 6 minutes. As the mixture begins to thicken, stir constantly.

3. Pull mixture off the heat after another minute or two, when it resembles the thickness of loose pudding. It will continue to thicken as it cools.

4. Strain through a sieve into a stainless steel bowl. Set the bowl in a larger bowl of ice water and stir occasionally, until mixture is cool. Use immediately or cover surface with plastic wrap to prevent a film from forming and chill in the refrigerator until needed. May be made 1 day in advance.

LOEWS
VENTANA CANYON RESORT
TUCSON

7000 North Resort Drive
Tucson, AZ 85750
800.234.5117
*www.loewshotels.com/
tucson*

Golf Courses:
Mountain, Canyon

Designer: Tom Fazio

Available holes: 36

Accommodations:
398 guestrooms,
including 27 suites

Rates: $–$$$$

Other Activities: Spa,
fitness center, tennis,
hiking, biking

The chiseled stone structure looks as if it was carved out of the rugged Santa Catalina Mountains, blending naturally into the desert setting. Warm earth tones and southwestern furnishings create an environment that is both rustic and elegant at the same time. A two-story glass wall overlooks the turquoise pool to the saguaro-studded mountain beyond. It's impossible to pass through the lobby without stopping to admire this visual masterpiece.

Guests may alternate days at the Fazio Mountain and Canyon courses, each offering the finest in Arizona golf. A 7,000 square foot spa and tennis center provides diversions for the non-golfer. Adventurous guests might opt for a package that includes hiking, biking, or hot air ballooning. There is something to appeal to everyone in this Sonoran Desert playground.

Active days mean hearty appetites, and Loews Ventana Canyon excels in fresh, imaginative American and Southwestern cuisine. If dressing for dinner, then choose the fine dining Ventana Room, and enjoy the city lights of Tucson twinkling in the background. Ranked top in the Southwest by *Condé Nast Traveler* and top in Tucson by *Zagat,* the new American cuisine delights even the most discriminating gourmand. The flagstone, copper, and leather interior of the Flying V Bar & Grill is as attractive as the southwestern-influenced plates emerging from the kitchen. Mesquite grilled steaks are a specialty as is the lengthy tequila menu. Mountain and pool views abound in the casual Canyon Café, serving a lavish brunch on Sunday in addition to daily breakfast, lunch and dinner.

Breakfast Menu

- HUEVOS RANCHEROS WITH ASADERO & TOMATILLO SALSA

ROASTED BREAKFAST CHIVE POTATOES

Dinner Menu

- SHRIMP ESCABÉCHE

MESQUITE-GRILLED STRIP LOIN WITH CHIMICHURRI

CORN-FRIED NOPALITOS
OR
RICOTTA & PROSCIUTTO RAVIOLI WITH CHANTERELLES

- APRICOT GINGER SEA BASS WITH TATSOI

- BLUE CHEESE & MUSHROOM BREAD PUDDING

- VANILLA BEAN CRÈME BRÛLÉE IN PUFF PASTRY

- *Recipe included*

Golf Pro's Tip

The mountains have an impact on golf shots. The putts will break quickly toward the city, away from the mountains.

Signature Hole

Mountain course, Number 3 — plays across 107 yards of cactus and canyons, offering desert wilderness views that stretch for miles south across the Sonoran Desert.

Huevos Rancheros

WITH ASADERO & TOMATILLO SALSA

The ancho is the dried form of the mild poblano chile, often used in chile rellenos. Asadero is a Mexican cheese made from cow's milk, very similar to a young California Monterey Jack cheese, with wonderful melting properties. This dish is full of flavor from the earthy, mildly spicy anchos and the tangy tomatillo salsa. It's quite striking on the plate, too.

SERVES 4

3 ancho chiles
1 cup boiling water
½ teaspoon cider vinegar
6 ounces chorizo bulk sausage
1 (15-ounce) can black beans, undrained
8 eggs

Salt and freshly ground black pepper
8 corn tortillas, warmed
1½ cups (6 ounces) grated Asadero or Monterey Jack cheese
1½ cups Tomatillo Salsa (recipe follows)
4 springs cilantro

1. Remove stems and seeds from ancho chiles. It's a good idea to wear disposable latex gloves to protect your hands from the heat of the chiles. Toast chiles in a dry skillet over medium heat until fragrant, about a minute or so. Place chiles in a bowl and cover with boiling water mixed with the vinegar. Rehydrate for 20 to 30 minutes. Purée chiles in a blender with just enough of the soaking liquid to make a thick paste (think tomato paste consistency). You need about ¼ cup of chile paste.

2. Cook chorizo in a skillet over medium heat until done, about 8 to 10 minutes. Drain and mix with beans (and their liquid) and ¼ cup ancho chile paste. Keep warm.

3. Cook eggs any style (fry, scramble, or poach) and season with salt and pepper.

4. Place 2 warm tortillas on a plate. Top with ½ cup of chorizo mixture. Top with eggs and sprinkle with ½ cup grated cheese. Top with ¼ cup of Tomatillo Salsa (recipe follows) and garnish with a sprig of cilantro. Repeat process for each plate.

Tomatillo Salsa

*C*hoose medium-size, firm tomatillos that have tight papery husks. It's not really an unripe (green) tomato, although it belongs to the same family. Salsa Verde (green salsa) is usually made with cooked tomatillos.

MAKES 1½ CUPS

1 jalapeño
12 tomatillos (about ¾ pound),
    papery husks removed

1 avocado
1 cup loosely packed cilantro leaves
Salt and freshly ground black pepper

1. Bring a large pot of water to boil. Meanwhile, roast the jalapeño over an open fire or in a skillet until the skin blisters. Place pepper in a plastic bag to steam for 5 minutes. Wearing protective latex gloves, scrape the skin off the pepper. Remove the seeds if desired (I like hot salsa, so I leave some of the seeds in). Rough chop the pepper and place in a food processor.

2. Wash and dry the tomatillos. Gently boil tomatillos until they begin to soften, about 3 to 4 minutes. Drain and add to the food processor with the jalapeño.

3. Cut the avocado in half and remove the pit. Scoop out the flesh and add to the food processor.

4. Add the cilantro leaves to the processor. Process mixture using the pulse button a few times, keeping it chunky. Season with salt and pepper. May be prepared 8 hours in advance. Store covered in the refrigerator, but bring to room temperature before using.

Shrimp Escabéche

*E*scabéche originated in Spain, and consisted of poached fish marinated overnight in a spicy sauce. Here the chef adds a southwestern twist, creating a chunky gazpacho-like shrimp cocktail that looks great served in a margarita glass and garnished with a lime wheel. I added a cooked jumbo (U-8) shrimp to the rim of the glass for another appetizing touch. (See photograph on page P-9.)

SERVES 4

1 tablespoon olive oil
½ pound (26/30 count) fresh shrimp, peeled, deveined
1 teaspoon minced garlic
1½ cups tomato juice
½ cup V-8® juice
2 tablespoons red wine vinegar
½ teaspoon Worcestershire sauce
12 drops hot sauce (such as Tabasco®)
½ cup peeled, seeded, and chopped cucumber
¼ cup finely chopped red onion

2 tablespoons chopped fresh cilantro
2 teaspoons drained capers
1 jalapeño pepper, seeded and minced
1 cup seeded, chopped red tomatoes
1 cup seeded, chopped yellow tomatoes (or yellow bell pepper)
Pinch sugar
Salt and freshly ground black pepper
1 avocado, peeled and chopped
1 lime, cut crosswise into ¼-inch wheels

1. Heat olive oil in a skillet over medium heat. Stir in shrimp and garlic. Cook, stirring frequently, until shrimp is pink and done, about 4 minutes. Chill.

2. Stir the next 12 ingredients (tomato juice through yellow tomatoes) together. Season with pinch of sugar, salt and pepper.

3. Layer the following in a margarita or beer glass.
  • ¼ cup tomato mixture
  • 2 tablespoons avocado
  • 2 to 3 pieces of shrimp

Repeat layers, ending with a touch of tomato mixture. Garnish with a lime wheel.

Apricot Ginger Sea Bass

*T*his recipe was originally prepared with black sea bass, which are found all along the U.S. Atlantic coast, but are now in danger of being depleted through overfishing. Striped sea bass is similar, and is plentiful, so I've made the switch. The resort serves this moist, semi-firm white fish on top of mashed potatoes, and garnishes the fish with sautéed crab, and tatsoi, a peppery Asian green, tossed with soy vinaigrette.

SERVES 4

½ cup water
¼ cup brandy
1 tablespoon soy sauce
1 teaspoon peeled and grated
    fresh ginger
¼ cup (1 ounce) chopped
    dried apricots

1 tablespoon olive oil
Salt and freshly ground
    black pepper
4 (6-ounce) striped sea bass
    fillets, skin removed

1. Bring water, brandy, soy sauce, and ginger to a boil in a small saucepan. Stir in apricots and reduce heat to a gentle simmer. Cook until apricots are soft, about 5 minutes, stirring occasionally. Purée mixture in a blender to make a glaze for the fish. (CAUTION: Cover lid with a towel, and apply pressure on the lid before turning the machine on, as hot liquid shoots straight up with considerable force. If you're not careful, you can burn yourself, or at least make a huge mess!) May be prepared 1 day in advance. Store covered in the refrigerator.

2. Heat oven to 350°F. Heat olive oil in an ovenproof skillet over medium-high heat. Season fillets on both sides with salt and pepper. When very hot, place fillets, flesh-side down. Shake pan to keep from sticking, and sear until lightly golden, about 2 to 3 minutes. Flip fish over, brush liberally with apricot glaze, and place in oven to finish cooking, about 5 to 7 minutes for medium temperature on a 1-inch thick fillet. While fish is cooking, bring remaining glaze to a boil in a small saucepan over medium-high heat. Boil 1 minute and remove from heat. Brush fillets once more with glaze just before serving.

Tatsoi

WITH SOY VINAIGRETTE

A cool weather green originally from Asia, tatsoi is also known as rosette bok choy. The resort gets its organic tatsoi from a local farmer in Tucson. Ask your specialty grocery to locate some for you. It has a lovely peppery mustard flavor. If you don't ask, you'll never get to try new things. If you still can't get your hands on tatsoi, no matter how nice you ask, substitute watercress to toss with this vinaigrette. This recipe is a garnish for the preceeding bass recipe.

SERVES 4

2 tablespoons soy sauce
1 tablespoon rice wine vinegar
1 teaspoon dark sesame oil
¼ cup olive oil

Salt and freshly ground black pepper
4 cups (4 ounces) tatsoi or
   watercress

1. Whisk soy sauce with rice wine vinegar and sesame oil. Slowly whisk in olive oil.

2. Season with salt and pepper. Toss with tatsoi.

B.Hillis

Blue Cheese & Mushroom Bread Pudding

Yes, it's as delicious as it sounds. It's attractive, too, because it's baked in individual ramekins, so the presentation is impressive. If you can't find fresh chanterelles, try fresh shiitakes (or you could rehydrate some dried chanterelles). This savory pudding is very rich, so serving it with a light fish entrée as the resort does makes a lot of sense.

SERVES 6

4 cups (about 8 slices, crusts removed) cubed sourdough bread
4 cups (about 8 slices, crusts removed) cubed white bread
1 tablespoon olive oil
1 cup chopped fresh chanterelles or shiitake mushroom caps
1 teaspoon minced garlic

¼ cup finely chopped fresh herbs (thyme, rosemary, oregano, etc.)
2 eggs, beaten
2 cups heavy cream
¼ cup crumbled Roquefort or other blue cheese
Salt and freshly ground black pepper

1. Heat oven to 400°F. Spread bread cubes on 2 baking pans with sides and lightly toast in the oven for 3 to 5 minutes. Remove to cool, leaving oven on. Spray 6 (8-ounce) custard cups or ramekins with nonstick spray.

2. Heat olive oil in a skillet over medium-high heat. Add mushrooms and garlic. Cook, stirring occasionally, until mushrooms are tender, about 3 to 4 minutes. Stir in fresh herbs. Season with salt and pepper. Set aside.

3. Whisk eggs and cream together in a large mixing bowl. Mix in mushrooms and blue cheese. Quickly mix in bread cubes.

4. Divide mixture evenly between custard cups. Place cups in a large roasting pan. Place pan in oven and pour in enough hot water to come halfway up the sides of the cups.

5. Bake, covered with foil, until almost set, about 25 minutes. Remove foil and cook another 5 to 10 minutes, until tops are crusty and light golden brown. Remove and cool 5 to 10 minutes before serving.

Vanilla Bean Crème Brûlée

IN PUFF PASTRY

Not all crème brûlées are baked, apparently. This is a custard cooked completely on top of the stove, chilled, then poured into golden puff pastry shells. Getting the burnt sugar crust is a challenge, but who doesn't love a good challenge in the kitchen? You can also serve these in regular custard cups or ramekins and then the torching is easy.

SERVES 4

4 frozen puff pastry shells, thawed
8 egg yolks
⅓ cup sugar
½ vanilla bean, split

2¼ cups heavy cream
4 tablespoons sugar
1½ cups fresh berries
Mint sprigs

1. Follow directions of puff pastry package and bake shells. Remove from oven and gently remove the top of each shell to create a "bowl." Cool completely. Place on a small sheet pan that will fit in your refrigerator.

2. Whisk the egg yolks with the sugar in the top of a double boiler set over barely simmering water. Continue whisking constantly, scraping the eggs to prevent them from scrambling until the mixture is thick and lemon-colored, about 8 to 10 minutes (a really good workout for your arm). Remove from heat and set aside.

3. Scrape the seeds of the vanilla bean into a saucepan. (Save the vanilla bean for flavoring sugar or discard.) Pour in the cream. Place over medium heat and bring just to a boil. Remove from heat.

4. Whisk a little hot cream into the egg yolk mixture to warm the eggs before whisking in the rest of the hot cream.

5. Place the double boiler back over simmering water and cook the egg and cream mixture until thick, whisking frequently, about 8 to 10 minutes. If you run your finger across the back of the spoon, the path your finger creates should stay clean. If the sauce runs through the path, it's not thick enough, and needs to cook a little more.

6. Strain mixture through a fine sieve into a bowl. Set that bowl in a larger bowl filled with ice water. Stir to cool. When custard is cold to the touch, divide evenly between the 4 puff pastry bowls, filling as full as you can without spilling. Chill in the refrigerator, uncovered until firm, about 2 hours. May be prepared up to 8 hours in advance. Cover after 2 hours and keep chilled until ready to serve.

7. Sprinkle the tops of the custards with a generous tablespoon of sugar. Use a kitchen blowtorch and burn the sugar. Keep the torch flame focused on the center of the custard so that the edges of the puff pastry don't burn too much. If you use regular custard cups, you can burn the sugar under a preheated broiler for about 1 to 3 minutes. Serve with fresh berries.

CRÈME BRÛLÉE VS. CRÈME CARAMEL
VS. FLAN VS. POT DE CRÈME

All of these desserts begin as a basic custard mixture of either egg yolks or whole eggs, or a combination of both; milk or cream or a combination; sugar, and other flavorings. Crème Brûlée, Crème Caramel and Flan involve caramelized sugar as well. All four of these desserts are baked in a water bath to ensure slow, even cooking.

Crème Brûlée is translated from French to English as "burnt cream." Most crème brûlées are made with egg yolks, not whole eggs. Individual ramekins or custard cups are filled with the custard mixture and baked until jelled. Once cooled and chilled, the top is sprinkled with sugar that is then melted and caramelized to a dark, dark brown under a broiler or with a blowtorch. The thin layer of burnt sugar hardens and becomes delicately crisp, contrasting nicely with the smooth, cream custard beneath. Some people like to use a special brûlée dish that is wider and shallower than a ramekin, creating more surface space for the crisp sugar crust.

Crème Caramel, served in individual ramekins, starts with caramelized sugar on the bottom and the custard on top. After baking, the dessert is cooled and chilled. A thin knife blade slipped around the inside of the ramekin loosens the custard before it is turned upside down onto a dessert plate. The ramekin is removed to expose the caramel layer that that is now on top of the custard.

Flan is very similar to crème caramel, but the traditional Spanish recipe calls for condensed or evaporated milk. Sometimes it is baked in a larger dish, not individual ramekins. Otherwise it is the same as crème caramel, baked with the caramel layer on the bottom, but inverted before serving so that the caramel is on top.

Pot de Crème is related to all three previous desserts. The difference is that no caramel is used and the cooking vessel is different. Pot de Crème may be made with egg yolks, or a combination of egg yolks and whole eggs. The name translates to "pot of cream," and the French traditionally baked these custards in little porcelain cups with lids. Melted chocolate is often added to the custard before baking.

THE PHOENICIAN

Scottsdale

6000 East
Camelback Road
Scottsdale, AZ 85251
800.888.8234
www.thephoenician.com

Golf Courses: Oasis/
Desert/ Canyon

Designers: Homer Flint/
Ted Robinson, Sr./
Robinson & Flint

Available holes: 27

Accommodations: 654
guestrooms, including
suites, casitas, and villas

Rates: $$$–$$$$

Other Activities: Centre
for Well-Being Spa, tennis,
shopping, art collection,
cactus garden

Grand opulence doesn't even begin to describe this stunning Phoenician resort. Rocky Camelback Mountain rises in the background of the tiered main hotel. Arizona's only Mobil Five-Star resort is nothing short of a small village, an oasis in the desert for the well-heeled. A multi-million dollar art collection adorns the interior and grounds of the hotel, with life-size sculptures from the late Allan Houser and other magnificent art from renowned American, Asian, and European artists. Eleven grand pianos are spaced throughout the resort, and a wing of chic boutiques with art galleries, clothing, jewelry, and other specialty stores adds to the ritzy ambiance.

Three nine-hole, impeccably manicured golf courses, each named for its surrounding landscape — Desert, Canyon, and Oasis — combine to create different options for those seeking an 18-hole round of golf. While they are not considered "target" golf, as many Arizona courses are, there are plenty of challenges to negotiate to keep the ball out of natural desert habitat, especially on the Desert and Canyon courses. Oasis, as its name implies, is a lush, tropical setting with ample water.

The real star at this resort is the dining, and specifically Mary Elaine's, the Mobil Five-Star, AAA Five-Diamond, and Wine Spectator's Grand Award recipient. A tiny footstool at each table for purses is one of many examples of how attention to detail parlays into the ultimate dining experience. Refined French food with Mediterranean accents coupled with a three million-dollar wine cellar, seal Mary Elaine's status as the crown jewel of dining destinations in Arizona.

The other dining options are worthy of praise, too, especially the Terrace Dining Room and its lavish Sunday Champagne Brunch as well as Windows on the Green, the resort's Southwestern option with lovely views of the Oasis course.

Breakfast Menu

- MELON & YOGURT FRAPPÉ

- DRIED FRUIT & BERRY MUESLI

- VEGETABLE EGG WHITE FRITTATA
  WITH PARMESAN CHEESE

Dinner Menu

- GRILLED EGGPLANT
WITH HERBED GOAT CHEESE & MIXED GREENS

- LASAGNA OF FRENCH MUSHROOMS & LOVAGE
WITH FAVA BEAN COULIS

- CHILLED RHUBARB & STRAWBERRY COMPOTE

- PRICKLY PEAR MARGARITA

- *Recipe included*

Golf Pro's Tip

Putts break away from Camelback Mountain on both the Desert and Canyon courses.

Signature Hole

Desert course, Number 8 — this par 3 features elevated tees, built by hand on the southern slope of Camelback Mountain. The severely sloping green sits below the player and does not play to its 140-yard length.

Melon and Yogurt Frappé

"*F*rappé" is Italian for milkshake, and the tiny amount of coconut milk in this recipe gives the drink creaminess without a lot of fat and calories. The riper the melons, the better this frothy beverage tastes. The berries provide the color. For a pink drink, choose only red fruits. Blueberries and blackberries will shade the drink purple.

SERVES 2

½ cup peeled and chopped chilled honeydew
½ cup peeled and chopped chilled cantaloupe
¾ cup chilled pineapple juice
⅔ cup plain yogurt

⅓ cup assorted berries, fresh or frozen
2 tablespoons coconut milk
1 tablespoon honey
2 whole strawberries for garnish

1. Place all ingredients in a blender and Purée until smooth.

2. Pour into chilled glasses and garnish with a fresh strawberry.

Dried Fruit and Berry Muesli

*T*his is so much better than any muesli I've had in Europe. (OK, so I've only been there a couple of times, but I tasted lots of oatmeal mush, and this one is, by far, the best.) It's cool and creamy, with a nice crunch from the nuts and fruit. Start the night before you plan to serve it because the oats need to soak overnight.

SERVES 4

2 cups old-fashioned oats
Cold water
1 cup nonfat milk
½ cup honey
½ cup plain yogurt

½ cup assorted toasted nuts*
½ cup assorted dried fruits
⅛ teaspoon cinnamon
½ cup seasonal fresh berries

1. Place the oats in a container and with just barely enough cold water to cover the oats. Stir and cover container. Refrigerate overnight.

2. Mix soaked oats with milk, honey, yogurt, nuts, dried fruits, and cinnamon.

3. Divide mixture evenly between 4 bowls. Garnish with fresh berries.

Use a mixture of pecans, walnuts, almonds, and/or hazelnuts. To toast nuts, see page 18 under Common Procedures.

Vegetable Egg White Frittata
WITH PARMESAN CHEESE

I always assume that if a dish is low in fat and calories, it's more than likely low in flavor, too. Usually, I'm right. This time, I'm wrong. I think you'll like this open-faced omelet as much as I do. The cucumber and tomato side adds a tangy flavor, as well as some crunch. It's easy to use two pans if you want to double this recipe.

SERVES 2

4 or 5 broccoli florets
  (about ½ ounce)
¼ cup white or brown sliced
  mushrooms (about ½ ounce)
¼ of a small red bell pepper
  (about ½ ounce), thinly sliced
¼ cup fresh spinach (about ¼ ounce)
6 egg whites (or 6 ounces of
  egg substitute)

¼ teaspoon salt
Pinch freshly ground
  black pepper
1 tablespoon thinly sliced fresh
  basil leaves
1 teaspoon finely chopped chives
1 tablespoon grated Parmesan cheese
Cucumber & Tomato Salad
  (recipe follows)

1. Heat oven to 350°F. Steam the broccoli, mushrooms, bell peppers, and spinach, starting first with the broccoli, then adding the other vegetables. Keep adding the vegetables to the steamer in the order listed. It should only take about 4 minutes for the broccoli, 3 for the mushrooms, 2 for the red bell pepper, and 1 minute for the spinach. Remove and finely chop the bell pepper.

2. Lightly whip egg whites with a whisk until foamy, about 30 seconds, and season with salt and pepper. Heat an ovenproof nonstick 8-inch skillet over low heat.

3. Spray skillet with nonstick spray and add the egg whites. Sprinkle the top evenly with the steamed vegetables and let cook, lifting the edges of the frittata with a spatula occasionally to let the egg whites flow underneath, but without really stirring.

4. After 4 or 5 minutes, finish the frittata in the oven until eggs are completely cooked, about 2 to 3 more minutes. Sprinkle with herbs, Parmesan, and garnish with a tablespoon or so of the Cucumber & Tomato Salad.

Cucumber & Tomato Salad:

2 Roma tomatoes (about 6 ounces)
½ hothouse cucumber (about 7 ounces)
1 tablespoon thinly sliced fresh
  basil leaves
1 teaspoon sherry or cider vinegar
Salt and freshly ground black pepper

1. Core tomatoes and cut in half lengthwise. Cut each half into 3 equal pieces (half-moons).

2. Cut the cucumber half in half lengthwise. Cut into half-moons, about ½-inch thick.

3. Toss tomatoes and cucumbers with the basil and vinegar. Season with salt and pepper.

Grilled Eggplant

WITH HERBED GOAT CHEESE & MIXED GREENS

*W*ow! Paired with a glass of champagne, this incredible appetizer is one of my favorite recipes in the book. Even if you're not a huge eggplant fan, this dish will surely delight you. I'm one of those chefs who prefer to salt-soak eggplant to remove its bitterness. I know some chefs who don't think it makes a difference. It really is a matter of personal preference. You can experiment yourself to see which you prefer. (See photograph on page P-10.)

SERVES 4

Marinated Eggplant:
1 small (1 pound) eggplant
1 tablespoon salt
2 tablespoons olive oil
2 teaspoons minced garlic
Freshly ground white pepper

Herbed Goat Cheese:
$\frac{1}{4}$ cup (2 ounces) quality goat cheese
$\frac{1}{4}$ cup (2 ounces) cream cheese
1 teaspoon minced garlic

1 teaspoon finely chopped
  fresh chives
1 teaspoon finely chopped
  fresh thyme leaves

Mixed Greens:
1 cup mixed baby greens
4 teaspoons aged balsamic
  vinegar* divided
Salt and freshly ground
  white pepper

Eggplant and Goat Cheese:

1. Cut both ends off eggplant and discard. Cut remaining eggplant into 1-inch slices. Sprinkle both sides generously with kosher salt and place on a baking sheet in a single layer. Set aside for 30 minutes. Pat dry with paper towels, but do not rinse with water. Meanwhile, make the herbed goat cheese by mixing all the ingredients (goat cheese through thyme) together until smooth. Set aside at room temperature or keep in the refrigerator if making it far in advance.

2. Mix olive oil with garlic and brush on both sides of eggplant slices. Sprinkle with white pepper. Let marinate while grill is heating up.

3. Heat the grill to medium-high (375° to 400°F). Grill eggplant until soft, about 5 minutes per side. Alternatively, broil for 3 to 5 minutes on each side in a preheated broiler, about 3 inches from the heat source.

Mixed Greens:

1. Toss mixed greens with $1\frac{1}{2}$ teaspoons vinegar and season with salt and pepper.

2. Place a slice of grilled eggplant in the middle of 4 salad plates. Spread a tablespoon of goat cheese on top of each eggplant.

3. Place $\frac{1}{4}$ cup of dressed greens on top of each eggplant. Drizzle remaining balsamic over the top and around the plates, about $\frac{1}{2}$ teaspoon per plate.

*If you don't have a quality, aged balsamic, take $\frac{1}{2}$ cup of whatever balsamic vinegar you do have, and reduce it in a saucepan over medium-high heat until only $\frac{1}{4}$ cup remains. This will thicken and sweeten it by removing some of the water content.

Lasagna of French Mushrooms & Lovage

WITH FAVA BEAN COULIS

*I*f you normally think of lasagna as a big hunk of gut-filling pasta, smothered with tomato sauce, this elegant, petite plate will pleasantly surprise you. The flavors are delicate yet complex, in perfect harmony with each other. If you can't find lovage, which tastes similar to celery, substitute fresh celery leaves from the tender inner stalks. The resort uses a mixture of morels, chanterelles, and porcini mushrooms. It's difficult to find these mushrooms fresh, though they are widely available dry. I tend to prefer fresh mushrooms in this dish, so I use whatever exotic mushrooms I can find fresh.

SERVES 4

1 tablespoon olive oil
½ cup thinly sliced cipollini*
1½ teaspoons minced garlic
4 cups sliced assorted fresh
   exotic mushrooms
¼ cup heavy cream
2 tablespoons Devonshire cream**

¼ cup lovage leaves
   (or celery leaves)
1 tablespoon finely chopped chives
4 (2 x 10-inch) sheets of
   lasagna noodles
Salt and freshly ground black pepper
Fava Bean Coulis (recipe follows)

1. Heat olive oil in a skillet over medium heat. Stir in cipollini (or onions) and garlic, cooking until fragrant, about 1 minute. Stir in mushrooms and continue to cook until mushrooms are soft, about 4 to 5 minutes. (If you are using celery leaves instead of lovage, add them with the mushrooms.)

2. Pour in heavy cream and cook until heated through and mixture starts to thicken, about 2 minutes. Remove from heat and mix in Devonshire cream. Stir in lovage and chives.

3. Cook pasta in boiling salted water until al dente, about 7 to 8 minutes. Drain. Cut into 2-inch squares.

4. Place one piece of cooked pasta in the middle of a warm dinner plate. Top with a spoonful of mushroom mixture and spread to cover pasta. Top with another pasta layer and another spoonful of mushroom mixture, spreading to edges of pasta. Repeat once more, to have 3 layers of pasta, with a little mushroom mixture on top.

5. Drizzle Fava Bean Coulis around the lasagna.

*Cipollini is the baby bulb of an Italian hyacinth plant, with a mild, onion-like flavor. They look like little tiny bulbous spring onions. Difficult to find fresh? Yes, unless you're a 5-star resort. Substitute tiny fresh spring onions, or worst case, shallots, though you'll need to cut the portion in half. I did find a jar of cipollini marinated in balsamic vinegar on the Internet.

**Devonshire cream, a British specialty, is clotted cream, drained of most of its liquid. Clotted cream is made from unpasteurized milk gently heated and allowed to form a thick layer of cream on top. This cream is spooned off and labeled clotted cream. Substitute sour cream or crème fraîche, although both are more tangy than clotted cream.

Loews Ventana Canyon

Shrimp Escabèche

The Phoenician

Marinated Grilled Eggplant
with Herbed Goat Cheese &
Aged Balsamic

Barton Creek

Texas-Style Tortilla Soup

Hyatt Regency Coconut Point

*Braised Pineapple Rum Tart
with Pineapple Saffron Compote &
Blueberry Coulis*

Doral Golf Resort & Spa

Tropical Fruit Crêpes

Hyatt Regency Grand Cypress

Seared Ahi Tuna Salad with Citrus Coconut Vinaigrette

The Cloister at Sea Island

Grilled Chicken & Vegetable Spring Roll with Thai Chile Dipping Sauce

*Pinehurst
Resort*

*Chilled Blue
Crab Tower
with
Lemon Crème
Fraîche*

Fava Bean Coulis

*T*his recipe makes just enough to garnish the plates for the mushroom lasagna on the previous page. It makes a brilliant green sauce, a stark contrast to the earthy colors of the mushrooms and lasagna.

MAKES ½ CUP

1 tablespoon olive oil
1 tablespoon minced shallots
½ cup shelled fresh fava beans
 (from about ½ pound of pods)*

½ cup vegetable stock
½ cup (½ ounce) packed fresh
 spinach leaves
Salt and freshly ground black pepper

1. Heat the olive oil in a saucepan over medium heat. Stir in shallots and cook until fragrant, about 1 minute.

2. Stir in fava beans and continue to cook 2 minutes, stirring occasionally. Pour in vegetable stock and simmer for 5 minutes.

3. Remove pan from heat and stir in spinach. Cover for 1 minute. Pour mixture into a blender and Purée until smooth. Season with salt and pepper to taste. Keep warm until ready to use. May be made 1 day in advance. Store covered in the refrigerator. Gently reheat before serving.

* Seek out fresh instead of frozen fava beans. If you find small ones, you won't have to peel them after shelling them from the white pillows inside the tough pod. More than likely you'll find the larger ones that will need their outer bean skin removed. You can blanch them quickly in boiling water and dunk in ice water to help remove the skin, or, as I did, just make a little slit with a small knife at the point where the bean was attached to the pod, then peel with your fingers. It's a time consuming process, but you only need ½ cup, so it doesn't take that long. Besides, part of the fun of cooking is getting your hands on the food, right?

Chilled Rhubarb & Strawberry Compote

*T*his sprightly dessert qualifies as spa cuisine. I think it's important to have a fresh tasting dessert like this in your repertoire, because you can't have chocolate cake every day. Make the mint syrup first, even a few days ahead of time.

SERVES 4

1½ pounds rhubarb, leaves removed
  (or frozen, thawed)
2 cups (½ pound) strawberries,
  hulled (or frozen, thawed)
Zest of 2 oranges

6 sprigs of fresh mint, divided
3 cups water
2 tablespoons sugar substitute*
½ cup mint syrup
  (recipe follows)

1. Clean and cut the rhubarb (at an angle like celery for a stir-fry) into ½-inch pieces. You'll have about 5 cups of rhubarb. Cut the strawberries into quarters.

2. Place the orange zest and 2 sprigs of mint in a saucepan with the water. Bring to a boil. Stir in the rhubarb and bring back to a full boil.

3. Remove from heat and mix in the sugar substitute. Cool before stirring in the strawberries. Chill.

4. Scoop 1 cup into 4 chilled dessert bowls. Drizzle 2 tablespoons of mint syrup (recipe follows) on top of each bowl. Garnish with a sprig of mint.

Mint Simple Syrup:
½ cup sugar
⅓ cup water
1 cup chopped mint leaves and stems

1. Bring all ingredients to a boil, stirring frequently until sugar is dissolved.

2. Remove from heat, cool 30 minutes then strain, discarding mint. Chill.

3. May be made 1 week in advance. Store covered in the refrigerator.

*My friend Chef Cathy Rosenberg says Splenda® is the best sugar substitute, and the one she uses. She's cooked and baked with every sugar substitute on the market, from aspartame to stevia.

Prickly Pear Margarita

*U*niquely southwest, this vibrant pink and refreshingly sweet tart beverage is just what you need after a sunny round of golf. Stop in at the 19th hole, Windows on the Green, and sip this delightful desert drink. Prickly pear syrup is available in kitchen shops and grocery stores in Arizona, and you can find it on the Internet, too. See the Sources, page 204.

SERVES 1

3 tablespoons quality tequila
2 tablespoons Triple Sec
1 tablespoon Prickly pear syrup

½ cup fresh lemonade*
1 lime wedge

1. Pour all ingredients into a shaker or a blender. Mix well.

2. Salt the rim of a margarita glass (first dipped in a little lemonade or lime juice). Add ice and pour in margarita. Garnish with a lime wedge.

*Use your own recipe or here's mine: Heat ½ cup of sugar with ⅓ cup of water until sugar dissolves. Remove from heat and chill. Mix cooled sugar syrup with 1½ cups fresh squeezed lemon juice (from about 6 to 8 lemons) and 1½ cups of water. Chill.

B.Hillis

BARTON CREEK

8212 Barton Club Drive
Austin, TX 78735
800.336.6158
www.bartoncreek.com

Golf Courses: Fazio
Foothills/Fazio Canyons/
Crenshaw Cliffside/
Palmer Lakeside

Designers: Tom Fazio/
Ben Crenshaw/
Arnold Palmer

Available holes: 72

Accommodations:
300 guestrooms,
including 16 suites

Rates: $–$$$$

Other Activities: Spa,
fitness center, tennis,
indoor/outdoor pool

Texas has plenty of links, but only one capital of golf, Barton Creek, just minutes from downtown Austin. Western touches abound in this Hill Country resort, with cowhide furniture, rusty star sconces, and other chic cowboy touches, including old-timey black and white photos spread throughout, capturing the rural history of the area. No, cowboy boots are not allowed on the golf courses, but are frequently seen elsewhere, along with a few bolo ties and custom-made Stetsons.

Barton Creek earned the title of the capital of Texas golf, not because of its proximity to the state capitol, but because it offers 72 of some of the finest holes in the state. The Fazio-designed Foothills and Canyon courses are favorites among tall Texans as well as writers and editors of the top golf magazines. Native son Ben Crenshaw, a frequent player on all the courses as Barton Creek's touring professional, designed the Cliffside course with an eye toward maintaining the natural terrain.

The chefs maintain a true Texas flavor in the casual Austin Grill and the slightly more formal Hill Country Dining Room, overlooking the Fazio Foothills course. Texas beef is always on the menu, but so are rosemary lemon roasted free-range chicken, charbroiled, marinated veal loin, and even fresh fish presentations that surprise and delight, despite the land-locked location. Of course, lest one forgets where one is, the cowboy breakfast of gravy-smothered chicken fried steak with creamy grits should ring a bell, the Lone Star bell of Barton Creek, that is.

Dinner Menu

- BOCK BEER CHEESE SOUP

- TEXAS-STYLE TORTILLA SOUP

- GRILLED CHICKEN PECAN SALAD
WITH BLOOD ORANGE VINAIGRETTE

AUSTIN GRILL BARBECUE CHICKEN

- SOUTHERN-BRAISED MUSTARD GREENS

- WHIPPED POTATOES WITH ROASTED POBLANOS

- CARROT WALNUT CAKE

- PECAN & DARK CHOCOLATE TRUFFLES

- *Recipe included*

Golf Pro's Tip

The Fazio courses are both championship courses but play differently. Fazio Foothills offers small greens with subtle undulations while Canyons provides very large greens with more pronounced undulations. Play to your advantage by paying more attention to the direction of your approach shot at Foothills while concentrating more on the distance of your approach shot at Canyons.

Signature Hole

Fazio Foothills course, Number 18 — This picturesque par 5 requires players to avoid "Spelunker Bunker," a natural, spring-fed cave on the approach shot.

Bock Beer Cheese Soup

*M*y neighbor, Pat Johnston, said this was the best cheese soup he's ever had. He should know — he's tasted plenty of cheese soups as a former Campbell's Soup executive. I think it tastes best, like most soups, the next day. Barton Creek uses a Texas beer, Shiner Bock,® to make this soup. I actually found it at A. J.'s Fine Foods right here in Arizona. If you can't find it, just use another German-style bock beer, which will be dark, but not as dark as a stout beer.

SERVES 8

1 tablespoon olive oil
1 cup chopped onion
½ cup peeled and chopped carrot
½ cup chopped celery
1 jalapeño, seeded and chopped
4 cups chicken or vegetable stock
4 tablespoons butter
½ cup flour

2 (12-ounce) bottles bock beer
2 cups grated sharp cheddar cheese
1 cup heavy cream
1 tablespoon Worcestershire sauce
4 to 6 drops hot red pepper sauce
Salt and freshly ground
    black pepper
1½ cups seasoned croutons

1. Heat olive oil in a saucepan over medium-high heat. Stir in onions, carrot, celery, and jalapeño. Cook until onions are soft, about 3 to 4 minutes.

2. Pour in stock and bring to a boil. Meanwhile, cook a roux by melting the butter in a small skillet over medium heat. Whisk in the flour and cook until the roux darkens slightly and smells nutty, about 4 to 5 minutes. Whisk roux into boiling chicken stock mixture. Reduce heat to a simmer, cooking about 5 minutes to help cook out the starch flavor of the roux, stirring occasionally.

3. Pour in beer and bring back to a simmer. Cook, stirring occasionally for 5 minutes. Stir in cheddar cheese, stirring until cheese melts. Stir in cream, Worcestershire sauce, and hot sauce. Simmer 5 minutes. Purée with a hand held blender or in a regular blender in batches. (CAUTION: If you use a regular blender, fill only half full, cover lid with a towel, and apply pressure on the lid before turning the machine on, as hot liquid shoots straight up with considerable force. If you're not careful, you can burn yourself, or at least make a huge mess!)

4. Season with salt and pepper. Ladle into warmed soup bowls. Garnish with seasoned croutons.

Texas-Style Tortilla Soup

*H*earty, spicy, and chunky with chicken and vegetables, this is not your typical tortilla soup, though it has many of the same flavors. I can't wait to make this for my sister-in-law, Tish, who loves tortilla soup. We like very spicy foods, so I leave the seeds in the jalapeño. If you take them out, it really tones down this soup. The resort garnishes the top with red, white, and blue fried tortilla strips. I could only find white and yellow fresh corn tortillas, which I cut into very thin strips. To add some color, I dusted them with chile powder after frying them for a minute or so in 350°F canola oil. (See photograph on page P-11.)

SERVES 6

1 tablespoon butter
1½ cups chopped onion
1 tablespoon minced garlic
2 cups corn kernels (fresh or frozen)
1 cup seeded and chopped tomato
1 jalapeño, seeded and minced
2 (4-ounce) cans chopped mild
  green chiles
1 tablespoon cumin
1 tablespoon ancho chile paste*
2 teaspoons Mexican oregano**
2 teaspoons chile powder

¼ teaspoon ground white pepper
6 cups chicken stock
3 cups chopped cooked chicken
  breast (about ¾ pound)
¼ cup chopped cilantro
3 tablespoons cornstarch
2 tablespoons cold water

Garnish:
2 cups fried thin tortilla strips
3 large avocados, peeled and chopped
6 tablespoons sour cream

1. Melt butter in a stockpot over medium heat. Stir in onions and cook 2 minutes, stirring occasionally. Stir in garlic. Cook, stirring frequently, until onions are soft, about 2 to 3 more minutes.

2. Stir in corn, tomatoes, jalapeño, green chiles, and spices, cooking another minute or so.

3. Stir in chicken stock. Increase heat to medium-high and bring to a boil. Reduce heat and simmer for 10 minutes. Stir in chicken and cilantro. Bring to a boil. Whisk cornstarch and water together. Whisk into boiling soup. Reduce heat and simmer for a few minutes. Taste and season with salt if needed.

4. Ladle into warm soup bowls. Garnish with fried tortilla strips, avocado chunks, and a tablespoon of sour cream.

To make ancho chile paste, see step 1 of the Huevos Ranchero recipe on page 98.

**Mexican oregano is not the same herb as the more common Mediterranean oregano. Look for Mexican oregano on the Mexican food aisle of your grocery store or see Sources, page 206, for ordering information.*

Grilled Chicken & Pecan Salad

*T*he best part about cooking? Watching someone's face light up while eating something that they never would have guessed was that good. I was fortunate to have such a taster for this dish. Joe doesn't seem like the type to order a chicken salad. He looks like a steak sandwich guy, but he talked about this salad for weeks after trying it. There is nothing sissy about this salad, whether you serve it on a bed of lettuce dressed with the following Blood Orange Vinaigrette, or stuffed into a whole wheat pita.

SERVES 4

½ cup olive oil
1 tablespoon fresh chopped herbs
  (like thyme, rosemary, tarragon,
  basil, etc.)
1 tablespoon minced shallots
2 teaspoons minced garlic
½ teaspoon fresh ground
  black pepper
2 pounds chicken legs and thighs,
  with skin

2 tablespoons finely chopped carrots
2 tablespoons finely chopped
  red onion
2 tablespoons finely chopped celery
1 tablespoon mayonnaise
1 tablespoon honey
1 tablespoon Dijon mustard
½ teaspoon fresh thyme leaves
½ cup chopped toasted pecans
Salt and freshly ground black pepper

1. Whisk olive oil with 1 tablespoon fresh chopped herbs, shallots, garlic, and black pepper. Pour over chicken, turning to coat. Refrigerate for at least 1 hour, up to 8 hours.

2. Heat a grill to medium (350°F). Drain chicken from marinade. Grill (watch out for flare-ups from the oil on the chicken) until done, about 10 to 12 minutes on each side.

Remove from grill and cool enough to handle. Remove skin and bones.

3. Coarsely chop meat. Toss with the next 7 ingredients (carrots through thyme) until blended. Taste and season with salt and pepper. Sprinkle with pecans before serving. Store covered in the refrigerator, up to 3 days.

Blood Orange Vinaigrette

*T*he flesh of a blood orange is a stark, dark magenta, and the juice turns vivid hot pink when mixed with the oil in this vinaigrette. It's beautiful as well as sweet and tart.

MAKES 1 CUP

¼ cup blood orange juice
   (about 2 small oranges)
2 tablespoons white balsamic
   (or white wine) vinegar
1 tablespoon honey

1 tablespoon Dijon mustard
Pinch salt and freshly ground
   black pepper
½ cup vegetable oil (not olive)

1. Whisk blood orange juice through black pepper together.

2. Slowly drizzle in oil while whisking. Use a blender for a thicker, creamier consistency.

3. Taste and adjust seasonings. Store covered in the refrigerator, up to 4 days.

Southern-Braised Mustard Greens

I grew up eating braised greens. I never really liked them, but that's because they weren't as good as these. (Sorry Mom!) The vinegar and a touch of sugar really take the bitterness away and of course, the smoky bacon taste is classic Southern. There isn't much we can do about the awful dull green color of these greens, but after one flavor-bursting bite, who cares?

SERVES 4 TO 6

3 strips bacon, chopped
1 cup chopped onion
1 teaspoon minced garlic
¼ cup white wine
3 pounds mustard greens, washed,
   stems removed, and chopped

2 cups chicken stock
2 tablespoons cider vinegar
1 tablespoon brown sugar
Salt and freshly ground black pepper

1. Cook bacon in a large, deep skillet or saucepan until crisp. Remove with a slotted spoon and reserve on a paper towel to drain.

2. Stir onions and garlic into bacon fat. Cook until onions are soft, about 3 to 4 minutes. Carefully pour in wine and reduce liquid until only a tablespoon is left, about a minute.

3. Stir in mustard greens, a few at a time, turning with tongs. Add more when the previous batch wilts and creates more room in the pan. When all mustard has wilted, stir in stock, vinegar, and brown sugar.

4. Bring to a boil, then reduce heat to a simmer and cover. Cook until greens are tender, about 30 to 35 minutes. Season with salt and pepper.

Whipped Potatoes

WITH ROASTED POBLANOS

*P*oblanos are fresh, dark green — almost black — chiles with a mild heat. These fire-roasted smoky chiles spice up ordinary mashed potatoes. The recipe calls for regular baking potatoes, but I also like to use the buttery Yukon gold potatoes.

SERVES 6

2½ pounds russet potatoes, peeled
    and cut into chunks
5 tablespoons butter
¾ cups milk or half-and-half

2 roasted, peeled, and seeded
    poblano chiles*
Salt and freshly ground
    black pepper

1. Boil potatoes in salted water until tender, about 20 minutes.

2. Melt butter with the milk in a saucepan over low heat while potatoes finish boiling.

3. Drain and mash potatoes. Stir in just enough warm butter and milk mixture to make potatoes smooth and creamy.

4. Chop roasted poblanos and stir into potatoes. Season with salt and pepper.

*To roast chiles, see page 18 under Common Procedures

Carrot Walnut Cake

*M*y neighbors served this cake at a casual dinner party with other neighbors (sans one piece that I needed to taste myself), and I received a call that evening about how it was the best homemade carrot cake they'd ever had. I pressed finely chopped walnuts into the sides for a beautiful finish, and it helped to hide my somewhat less than perfect frosting job.

SERVES 8

4 eggs
¾ cup vegetable oil
2 cups sugar
½ teaspoon salt
2 cups plus 2 tablespoons flour
4½ teaspoons cinnamon
¾ teaspoon baking soda
¼ teaspoon baking powder
1 pound peeled, shredded carrots
¾ cup coarsely chopped walnuts
1 cup finely chopped walnuts
  (optional)

Cream Cheese Frosting:
8 ounces cream cheese, room
  temperature
4 tablespoons butter, room
  temperature
½ teaspoon vanilla extract
1 cup powdered sugar

1. Heat the oven to 375°F. Whip the eggs with an electric mixer on high speed until light and frothy, about 1 minute. With the mixer running, slowly drizzle in the oil.

2. Turn the speed to low, and gradually whip in the sugar and salt, a little at a time.

3. Whisk the flour, cinnamon, baking soda, and baking powder together. Gently fold the flour mixture into the egg mixture with a spatula. Fold in the carrots and ¾ cup coarsely chopped walnuts just before the flour is fully incorporated.

4. Divide batter between 2 greased 8-inch cake pans. Bake until a toothpick inserted in the center comes out with just a few moist crumbs attached, about 25 to 30 minutes.

5. Remove from oven, cool in pan for 5 minutes, then turn out onto a rack and cool completely. Frost with cream cheese frosting.

To make the frosting:

1. Beat the cream cheese and butter together until well blended.

2. Mix in the vanilla and powdered sugar, mixing just until combined.

3. Frost cake now, or later. If using later, cover frosting and chill. Bring to room temperature before using.

Pecan & Dark Chocolate Truffles

*O*K, these have magic properties. They disappear. I mean, I set a plate of them in the refrigerator, intending to bag them up to distribute to neighbors and friends. I kept finding excuses not to put them in bags and before I knew it, voilá! Gone! Making them is a little messy, but the good news is that you don't have to make perfectly round ones. My lopsided ones tasted just as good as the few I did manage to make perfectly round.

MAKES 30 TRUFFLES

½ cup heavy cream
¼ teaspoon vanilla extract
3 tablespoons butter, softened
9 ounces semisweet chocolate, chopped

6 ounces semisweet chocolate, melted
2¼ cups finely chopped toasted pecans*

1. Bring cream and vanilla to a boil in a small saucepan over medium heat. Remove from heat and stir in butter and 9 ounces of chopped chocolate. Cover with plastic wrap and let sit for several minutes. Vigorously stir until the choclate and cream are blended into a smooth brown mass. Set aside and let cool to thicken. Speed up the process by chilling in the refrigerator, uncovered, for about 35 to 40 minutes. The consistency needs to be thick but moldable.

2. Transfer the mixture to a large pastry bag fitted with a large plain round tip. Pipe out chocolate drops about the size of cherries on a parchment-lined baking sheet.

Conversely, scoop teaspoon-size balls instead of piping with a pastry bag. Refrigerate to firm, about 3 hours.

3. Roll into balls between your hands (I use disposable latex gloves because the chocolate melts quickly, making your hands messy.) Dip balls into melted chocolate using a fork and then roll in pecans. Return to refrigerator to firm again.

4. Store in the refrigerator, covered, for up to 1 week (if they last that long). Serve chilled or at room temperature.

To toast nuts, see page 18 under Common Procedures.

The Southeast

5001 Coconut Road
Bonita Springs, FL 34134
941.444.1234
*www.coconutpoint.
hyatt.com*

Golf Course: Raptor Bay
Golf Club-Osprey (9)/
Hawk (9)/ Eagle (9, 2004)

Designer:
Raymond Floyd

Available holes: 18
(27 in 2004)

Accommodations:
450 guestrooms,
including suites

Rates: $$–$$$$

Other Activities: Spa,
fitness center, beach, pool
with water slide,
tennis, eco-tours

Southwest Florida is home to the youngest resort in Par Fork! Just 20 minutes north of Naples, Coconut Point opened in the fall of 2001 on 26 acres of lush tropical evergreens along the Gulf of Mexico. Migrating birds such as blue herons, egrets, and the once-threatened whooping cranes share the manicured lawns and gardens of the property. A boardwalk leads from Coconut Point to Estero Bay where the temperate waters of the Gulf lap the shore. A ten-minute ferry ride delivers guests to a private island beach, perfect for soaking up Florida sunshine, but it's the golf course that is the outstanding feature here.

Raptor Bay is the first golf course in the world to be certified by Audubon International as a Gold Signature Sanctuary. Signature certification is awarded only to golf courses which are designed, constructed, and maintained according to Audubon International's precise environmental standards. The course is a habitat for the bald eagle, gopher tortoises, and other wildlife and plant species native to the area. The physical design of the course also incorporates a balance between man and nature, with preserved natural buffers along the Bay and protection of Halfway Creek, a prized wetland feature. Sand-magnet golfers will be thrilled to know there are no artificial sand bunkers. That's not to say there isn't sand on the course. Native sandy areas dotted with palmetto palms are scattered alongside the fairways and near the greens. It's a stunning example of a course designed specifically with nature in mind.

The seaside feel of the course is carried through to the dining scene at the golf club and the resort. Fresh seafood plays a starring role in many of the dining venues. The resort offers a fine dining restaurant, Tanglewood, featuring global cuisine and overlooking reflecting pools and artfully sculpted gardens. Tarpon Bay is a casual indoor/outdoor restaurant where seafood is the star, featuring fresh oysters and stone crab claws. The following recipes represent Braxton's at the golf club.

Breakfast Menu

- Spicy Pumpkin Bread

- Banana Bread

Chicken & the Pig
with Chipotle Hollandaise

- Sweet Potato Corn Hash

Dinner Menu

- Lobster & Avocado Salad with Vine-Ripened Tomatoes

Culotte Steak with Grilled Andouille Sausage
& Salsas Rojo & Verde

- Saffron Rice

- Braised Pineapple Rum Tart
with Pineapple Saffron Compote

- *Recipe included*

Golf Pro's Tip

Bring your short game. The elevated greens are heavily undulated with lots of roll-offs and collection points. You'll need a variety of short strokes from putting to chipping to bump-and-run.

Signature Hole

Osprey course, Number 5, par 4 — a shimmering lake down the entire left side of the fairway and natural habitat on the right requires the tee shot to be accurate. Another lake comes into play just before the elevated green. The gorgeous view of Coconut Point in the background provides yet another distraction. Focus!

Spicy Pumpkin Bread

*T*ender, moist, and gingery, this is the best pumpkin bread recipe I've tried. It doesn't need dried fruit or nuts or anything else to make it better. It's perfect just the way it is.

MAKES 2 MEDIUM LOAVES

2 cups flour
2 cups sugar
¾ teaspoon baking soda
½ teaspoon salt
¾ teaspoon ground ginger
¾ teaspoon ground cinnamon

¾ teaspoon ground cloves
¾ teaspoon ground nutmeg
2 eggs
¾ cup vegetable oil
½ cup water
1 (15-ounce) can pumpkin purée

1. Heat oven to 350°F. Spray 2 medium (8½ x 4½ x 2½) loaf pans with nonstick spray.

2. Whisk first 8 ingredients (flour through nutmeg) together in a large bowl.

3. Beat the eggs with the oil, water, and pumpkin purée. Pour egg mixture over flour mixture and stir just to combine (a few lumps are fine).

4. Divide batter evenly between the pans and bake until a toothpick inserted in the center comes out with just a few moist crumbs attached, about 40 to 45 minutes. Cool a few minutes then turn out bread onto a rack and cool completely.

Banana Bread

I tried five banana bread recipes for this book, and liked this one the best. Tender, moist, and not too sweet, this recipe is a keeper. You could double the recipe, keep one, and share one. Did you get my address?

MAKES 1 STANDARD LOAF

1¾ cups flour
⅔ cup sugar
1¼ teaspoons cream of tartar
¾ teaspoon baking soda
½ teaspoon salt

2 eggs, lightly beaten
1 pound ripe bananas
  (about 1½ cups mashed)
6 tablespoons butter, melted

1. Heat oven to 350°F. Spray a standard loaf pan (9 x 5 x 3) with nonstick spray.

2. Whisk the first 5 ingredients (flour through salt) together in a large bowl.

3. Mix the beaten eggs and mashed bananas together. Pour egg mixture over the flour mixture and mix just to combine, stirring in the melted butter at the end.

5. Pour batter into pan and bake until golden brown on top and a toothpick inserted in the center comes out mostly clean, or with a few moist crumbs attached, about 40 to 50 minutes. Cool a few minutes then turn out bread onto a rack and cool completely.

Sweet Potato Corn Hash

H ere's a different twist on traditional breakfast hash. The sweet potatoes and corn make a great flavor combination. I used a mandoline (slicer) so that the potatoes would be uniform in size for even cooking and a better-looking dish. I also cut them small so that the cooking time was not more than 10 minutes. Cut them any larger than ¼-inch, and you'll need to increase the cooking time.

SERVES 4

2 tablespoons butter
1 cup chopped onion
1 pound sweet potatoes, peeled and
  cut into ¼-inch cubes

1½ cups corn kernels
  (fresh or frozen, thawed)
1 teaspoon fresh thyme leaves
Salt and freshly ground black pepper

1. Melt butter in a large skillet over medium heat. Stir in onions and sweet potatoes. Cook until potatoes are tender, about 10 minutes.

2. Stir in corn and thyme. Cook until corn is hot, about 2 to 3 minutes. Season with salt and pepper.

Chilled Lobster & Avocado Salad

*D*id you know that if you ask nicely, your butcher will cook your lobster for you? That way, you don't have to kill it yourself. By the way, culinary school and the great chefs at the Boulders Resort taught me that the humane way to kill a lobster is to plunge a knife in its head before dropping it in boiling water. See why I ask my butcher to help? Try this salad with grilled shrimp, too. I don't seem to have the same mental picture when grilling headless shrimp for some reason. This is a beautiful, mouthwatering salad, despite the graphic intro. Like the citrus segments, the Cabernet Port Vinaigrette is just a garnish, but you won't believe the additional flavor it adds. Make it in advance so that you'll have it ready when you make this beautiful salad.

SERVES 4

¼ cup finely chopped red onion
1 tablespoon lemon juice
½ cup water

2 (1-pound lobsters), boiled or
  steamed, shells removed

Lemon Cumin Vinaigrette:
¼ cup lemon juice
2 teaspoons ground cumin
Pinch cayenne pepper
Salt and freshly ground black pepper
½ cup extra virgin olive oil

Avocado salad:
2 ripe avocados
½ small head frisée lettuce, washed,
  dried, and torn into pieces
4 small vine-ripened tomatoes
  (about 1 pound) sliced ¼-inch thick
2 oranges, peeled and segmented
  (no pith)
1 grapefruit, peeled and segmented
  (no pith)
1 cup (5 ounces) grape tomatoes,
  cut in half
½ cup Cabernet Port Vinaigrette
  (recipe follows)

1. Toss the red onions with the 1 tablespoon of lemon juice and water. Let sit for 10 minutes. Drain and rinse onions twice.

2. Slice cooked lobster tail meat into ½-inch thick medallions. Keep medallions and claws chilled until ready to serve.

3. To make the Lemon Cumin Vinaigrette, whisk the ¼ cup of lemon juice with cumin, cayenne and season with salt and black pepper. May be prepared 1 day in advance. Chill covered.

4. Peel and chop the avocados. Toss with the drained red onions and 2 tablespoons of the lemon vinaigrette. Toss the frisée

with 2 tablespoons of the lemon vinaigrette.

5. To serve, lay 3 or 4 slices of tomato in the center of a chilled plate. Place a mound of frisée on top of tomatoes. Top with ¼ cup avocado mixture.

6. Toss chilled lobster with remaining lemon vinaigrette. Place 3 medallions on top of avocado. Lay orange and grapefruit segments around the lobster mound. Scatter a few grape tomato halves between the fruit segments.

7. Drizzle fruit and grape tomatoes with a 2 tablespoons of the Cabernet Port Vinaigrette. Garnish with a lobster claw.

Cabernet Port Vinaigrette:
(Makes ¾ cup)
1 cup Cabernet Sauvignon
1 cup ruby port
⅓ cup sugar
1 sprig fresh thyme
Salt and fresh ground black pepper
¼ cup olive oil

1. Bring Cabernet, port, sugar, and thyme to a boil in a saucepan over medium-high heat. When liquid is reduced to ½ cup, about 25 minutes, remove from heat. It will foam during the last few minutes, and you'll have to remove the pan from the heat to gauge how far it has reduced. Remove thyme sprig. Cool.

2. Place mixture in a blender, and with the blender running drizzle in the oil. Season with salt and pepper. May be made 3 days in advance. Chill covered, but return to room temperature to serve, as it thickens when chilled.

Saffron Rice

*T*he addition of capers and tangy kalamata olives takes this fragrant yellow rice to a sublime level. I could eat a plate of just this dish, and I practically did because my husband didn't want any. Jeff doesn't like olives but capers are OK. Go figure. Top with some toasted sliced almonds and you'll be in keeping with the Mediterranean motif.

SERVES 8

1¼ cups basmati rice
3 tablespoons butter, divided
½ cup chopped onion
Pinch of saffron
2½ cups hot chicken or
   vegetable stock
½ cup cream
¼ cup finely chopped red onion

¼ cup chopped kalamata olives
1 tablespoon capers, drained
1 tablespoon chopped fresh herbs
   (parsley, oregano, basil, etc.)
2 tablespoons grated
   Parmesan cheese
Salt and freshly ground
   black pepper

1. Rinse rice in water and drain. Repeat once more.

2. Melt 2 tablespoons of butter in a heavy-bottomed saucepan over medium heat. Stir in onions and pinch of saffron. Cook, stirring frequently, until onions are soft, about 3 to 4 minutes.

3. Stir in rice and cook, stirring frequently, until rice is well coated with butter, about 2 minutes.

4. Pour in stock and cream. Bring to a boil then reduce heat to low. Cover and cook until rice is done and liquid is absorbed, about 15 to 18 minutes.

5. Meanwhile, heat remaining 1 tablespoon of butter in a small skillet over medium heat. Stir in red onions and cook until soft, about 2 minutes. Mix in olives, capers, and herbs. Cook 1 minute.

6. Fluff rice with a fork. Toss in red onion mixture and Parmesan cheese. Season with salt and pepper. Serve warm.

Braised Pineapple Rum Tarts

WITH PINEAPPLE SAFFRON COMPOTE

*T*his is a gorgeous dessert, and you can make many of the components in advance so putting it together for a dinner party is no big deal. The pineapple and caramel ice cream were made for each other, a perfect balance of acidity and cream. I found a delicious caramel frozen yogurt called Dulce de Leche by Häagen Dazs. This recipe can easily be doubled. (See photograph on page P-12.)

SERVES 4

2 tablespoons butter
¼ cup brown sugar
¼ cup spiced or dark rum
4 (½-inch) slices of cored and peeled
   fresh pineapple
1 sheet puff pastry, almost thawed
1 egg yolk

1 tablespoon water
Pineapple Saffron Compote
   (recipe follows)
1 pint caramel ice cream (purchased)
Blueberry Coulis (recipe follows)
Fresh blueberries and mint
   for garnish

1. Melt the butter and brown sugar together in a large skillet over medium heat. Carefully stir in rum (remove pan from heat to pour in rum to avoid a flare-up). Add pineapple slices and cook about 4 minutes on each side. Cover and lower heat to simmer until tender, about 20 minutes, turning the pineapple once. This can be done 1 day in advance. Chill covered.

2. Heat the oven to 400°F. Cut out 4 circles from the almost thawed puff pastry sheet, slightly bigger than the diameter of the pineapple. Place circles on a baking sheet lined with parchment paper or a silicone mat.

3. Beat the yolk with the water. Brush only the tops (careful to avoid the sides) of the pastry circles with egg mixture. (Egg on the sides will prevent the pastry from rising in the oven.) Bake 7 to 10 minutes, until the

circles puff up and begin to turn golden brown. Remove pan from oven but leave oven on.*

4. Place a pineapple slice on top of each puff pastry and return to the oven and cook until puff pastry is golden brown, about 10 to 15 minutes. The weight of the pineapple will deflate the puff pastry somewhat.

5. Place a pineapple tart on a plate. Place a small scoop of caramel ice cream on top of the pineapple hole. Drizzle Pineapple Saffron Compote on top of and around tart. Dot plate with Blueberry Coulis. Garnish with fresh blueberries and mint.

*You may assemble tarts through step 3 earlier in the day, and finish with step 4 and 5 after you finish dinner, while clearing the plates. Just be sure to have the oven preheated to 400°F before you put the tarts back in the oven.

Pineapple Saffron Compote

*E*ven if you decide not to do the preceding recipe, please promise me you'll make this compote. It's excellent on vanilla ice cream and on toasted angel food cake. You won't be disappointed, I promise. The cracked black pepper is not a typo. It really adds another fun dimension to this luscious, tropical sauce.

MAKES 2 CUPS

1 cup sugar
½ cup orange juice
¼ cup spiced or dark rum
2 tablespoons water
Pinch of saffron

3 cups chopped fresh pineapple
    (about 1 pound)
¼ teaspoon freshly cracked black
    pepper (coarse grind)

1. Bring sugar, orange juice, rum, water, and saffron to a boil in a saucepan over medium-high heat. Cook until liquid reduces by half, about 5 to 8 minutes.

2. Stir in chopped pineapple and reduce heat to a simmer. Cook until pineapple is tender and mixture is syrupy, stirring occasionally, about 15 minutes. (The mixture foams up while cooking.) Remove from heat and stir in cracked pepper. Cover and chill. May be prepared up to 2 days in advance.

Blueberry Coulis

MAKES 1 CUP

2 cups blueberries (fresh or frozen)
½ cup sugar

2 tablespoons water (if using fresh
    blueberries)
1 teaspoon lemon juice

1. Bring blueberries, sugar, and water to a boil in a saucepan over medium heat. Reduce heat and simmer for about 5 minutes. Remove from heat and cool. Stir in lemon juice.

2. Strain solids, reserving liquid. Add solids to blender and just enough reserved liquid to make a sauce consistency. Purée until smooth. Add a little more reserved liquid if necessary. (I had about ¼ cup of liquid left, and my sauce was thick like ketchup.) Cover and chill. May be prepared up to 3 days in advance.

DORAL.
GOLF RESORT AND SPA

4400 NW 87 Avenue
Miami, FL 33178
877.893.6725
www.doralresort.com

Golf Courses: Blue
Monster/Great White/
Red/Gold/ Silver

Designers: Dick Wilson
& Raymond Floyd/Greg
Norman/Bob Van Hagge
& Raymond Floyd/
Dick Wilson/Devlin,
Hagge & Jerry Pate

Available holes: 90

Accommodations:
693 newly-renovated
guestrooms

Rates: $$–$$$$

Other Activities: Spa,
tennis, swimming,
children's camp,
shopping

Visiting Doral Golf Resort and Spa is like visiting a not-so-tiny kingdom, where loyal subjects pay homage to mystical masters — the Blue Monster and The Great White. This totally self-contained resort is only minutes from the Miami International Airport but fortunately feels isolated from the urban surroundings. Famed for offering 90 holes of golf, Doral is to golfers what Disney World® is to children — a required stop somewhere along the way.

The Spa part of this successful equation is also getting its share of recognition. Offering more than 100 spa services, the Tuscan-inspired structure is a consistent winner in the Zagat Survey and among Conde Nast Traveler's readers. The best part? The demonstration kitchen where the chef shares sensible cooking techniques, demystifying the "fat is bad" hyperbole. Pick up a copy of the Gourmet Spa Cuisine Recipe Collection, the resort's own cookbook, and recreate some of the flavor-packed healthful meals served at the Spa's peaceful Atrium Restaurant.

The resort offers several more dining options. Windows on the Green, as the name suggests, provides panoramic views of the 18th hole of the Blue Monster, while serving up original seafood creations with South Florida and Caribbean touches. Terrazza also provides golf course views along with casual café fare like old-fashioned meatloaf and club sandwiches. Champions Sports Bar and Grill serves a mean burger and hosts a popular happy hour. Bungalou's Bar & Grill located in the heart of the Blue Lagoon, the resort's million-gallon water park, is a poolside restaurant with a casual Caribbean atmosphere.

Breakfast Menu

- STRAWBERRY SPLASH FRUIT SMOOTHIE

- MIAMI SUNRISE FRUIT SMOOTHIE

- POWER PARFAIT

- WHOLE WHEAT PANCAKES WITH APPLE APRICOT COMPOTE

Dinner Menu

- TOMATO CROSTINI

- SPA POTATO SKINS

- GRILLED SEA BASS WITH CORIANDER SAUCE

- ASIAN STIR-FRY

- TROPICAL FRUIT CRÊPES

- *Recipe included*

Golf Pro's Tip

With 117 deep and penal bunkers on the Blue Monster and 222 pot bunkers on the Great White, you will need to bring your "A" game for these two courses.

Signature Hole

Blue Monster course, Number 18, par 4 — with the wind in your face, you need a long and accurate tee shot. Water comes into play on the second shot and bunkers lurk on the right near the wildly undulating green.

Strawberry Splash Fruit Smoothie

*W*hat a great way to get a serving of soy, which is so nutritionally important for women, especially. If you can't fathom the soy milk, try skim milk instead. The resort calculates the calories as 170 and only 1 gram of fat. Use very ripe strawberries and the color will be a striking pink.

SERVES 2

1 cup nonfat soy milk
1 small (4½ ounces) ripe banana
1 cup sliced strawberries, plus 2
   whole for garnish

¼ cup chopped pineapple
1 cup crushed ice
2 teaspoons honey

1. Place all ingredients (except whole strawberries) in a blender and purée until smooth.

2. Pour into 2 chilled glasses. Cut a slit in the 2 remaining strawberries from tip end. Place one strawberry on the rim of each glass.

Miami Sunrise Fruit Smoothie

*T*he taste is decidedly mango. Purée an 8-ounce, peeled and seeded ripe mango in a blender, or use canned mango nectar. This thick, creamy shake is a pretty pale yellow.

SERVES 2

1 cup nonfat soy milk
¾ cup mango purée
⅔ cup chopped pineapple,
   plus 2 wedges for garnish

1 cup crushed ice
2 teaspoons honey

1. Place all ingredients (except the pineapple wedges) in a blender and purée until smooth.

2. Pour into 2 chilled glasses. Garnish glasses with pineapple wedges.

Power Parfait

*T*he power part comes from calcium in the yogurt, protein in the cottage cheese, fiber in the wheat germ, and carbohydrates in the fruit. It's not too sweet and tastes a little nutty. It's attractive layered in a wineglass, too. You'll feel full, and will have consumed only 175 calories. Not a bad way to start your morning.

SERVES 1

¼ cup plain nonfat yogurt
1 teaspoon wheat germ
½ cup quartered strawberries
½ cup blueberries
¼ cup 1% milkfat cottage cheese

1 teaspoon wheat germ
¼ cup blackberries
¼ cup raspberries
1 pitted cherry (optional garnish)

1. Layer the ingredients in the order listed, starting with the yogurt in a large red wineglass. Top with cherry.

2. Chill until ready to serve.

Whole Wheat Pancakes

WITH APPLE APRICOT COMPOTE

*T*hese are spa pancakes. Can you tell by tasting? Yes, but only a little, and for those who want to have pancakes without the guilt, they're perfect. Nancy and Emmy, my tasters from the Seattle area, thought they were tender and flavorful, and Nancy was grateful for the low fat and calories. I thought they were especially good compared to some spa cakes I've tried. That apricot topping is sweet and spicy. I bet it would be good on top of real vanilla ice cream. We won't quote those calories.

SERVES 7

1 cup flour
1 cup whole wheat flour
1 tablespoon sugar
2 teaspoons baking powder
2 teaspoons baking soda
1 teaspoon salt

2 eggs
2 cups low fat buttermilk
1 tablespoon molasses
1 tablespoon butter, melted

1. Heat a large skillet or griddle over medium-low heat.

2. Whisk flours, sugar, baking powder, baking soda, and salt together in a large bowl.

3. Beat eggs with buttermilk and molasses. Pour egg mixture over flour mixture and mix just to combine. Stir in melted butter.

4. Spray skillet with nonstick spray and ladle ⅛ cup batter onto hot surface. Cook until bubbles form on surface and edges start to dry, about 2 minutes. Flip and cook another minute or so. This makes about 28 little silver dollar cakes. Serve 4 cakes per person. Top with Apple Apricot Compote.

Apple Apricot Compote:
¼ cup golden raisins
¼ cup chopped dried apricots
½ cup hot water
1 pound Granny Smith apples
¼ cup apricot nectar
3 tablespoons brown sugar
1 teaspoon cinnamon
⅛ teaspoon pinch nutmeg

1. Plump raisins and apricots in hot water for about 10 or 15 minutes.

2. Core but don't peel apples. Chop into ½-inch chunks.

3. Coat a skillet with nonstick spray and set over medium heat. Stir in apples and cook until tender, stirring occasionally, about 8 to 10 minutes.

4. Drain raisins and apricots, discarding water. Stir plumped fruit and remaining ingredients into the apples, cooking over low heat until soft and hot, about 5 minutes.

Tomato Crostini

$\mathcal{T}$his spa recipe is best when you use the ripest, most flavorful tomatoes you can find. If you're not concerned about the fat and calories, spread a little goat cheese on the baguettes before topping with the tomato mixture.

SERVES 8

2 pounds fresh tomatoes, seeded
   and chopped
2 teaspoons olive oil
2 tablespoons thinly sliced garlic
4 tablespoons thinly sliced fresh basil
Salt and freshly ground black pepper

24 slices (1 pound) thinly sliced
   French baguette
1 tablespoon chopped fresh basil
1 tablespoon chopped fresh oregano
1 tablespoon chopped fresh thyme
½ cup goat cheese (optional)

1. Toss the tomatoes with the olive oil, garlic, and basil slices. Season with salt and pepper. Cover and refrigerate overnight (a minimum of 4 hours). Drain mixture after marinating, discarding liquid.

2. Heat broiler or toaster oven. Spray bread slices lightly with nonstick spray. Toss chopped basil, oregano, and thyme

together. Sprinkle bread slices with the herb mixture and lightly toast. If using goat cheese, spread 1 teaspoon on each slice after toasting.

3. Spoon tomato mixture over toast and serve immediately, allowing 3 slices per person.

Spa Potato Skins

I don't care if these are spa skins. They're delicious — crispy shell, creamy melted cheese and a cool tang from the sour cream topped with oniony crunches. The fact that they're not loaded with fat and calories like traditional potato skins is just a bonus.

SERVES 4

2 baking potatoes (about 1¼ pounds)
¼ cup shredded low fat
    cheddar cheese

2 tablespoons low fat sour cream
2 tablespoons thinly sliced green
    onions (cut on the diagonal)

1. Heat oven to 400°F. Lightly prick potatoes with a fork a few times. Bake until almost done, about 40 minutes. Cool potatoes.

2. Slice lengthwise and scoop out flesh, leaving about ¼ inch of flesh. Reserve potato flesh for another recipe.

3. Cut each skin in half, crosswise, to yield 4 pieces per potato.

4. Reheat oven to 400°F. Lightly spray baking sheet and potato skins with

nonstick spray. Place skins on sheet and bake until crisp and golden brown, about 20 to 25 minutes.

5. Remove from oven, top each skin with ½ tablespoon of cheese. Return to oven to melt cheese, about 3 minutes.

6. Remove from oven and top each skin with 1 teaspoon each of sour cream and green onions.

Grilled Sea Bass
WITH CORIANDER SAUCE

*C*ertain species of sea bass, such as the Black sea bass, are in danger of being overfished. Striped sea bass is plentiful and worth seeking out. This recipe would be nice with halibut, too. The coriander sauce is delicate, with citrus and floral undertones. Don't make the sauce in advance. It tastes best as soon as it's made. Try this dish with the following recipe, a colorful Asian stir-fry.

SERVES 4

4 (6-ounce) sea bass fillets
Juice of 2 limes (about $\frac{1}{3}$ cup)
1 teaspoon minced garlic
3 tablespoons chopped parsley
2 tablespoons butter
1 hothouse cucumber
   (about 12 ounces)

Salt and freshly ground
   black pepper
Coriander sauce
   (recipe follows)
1 lemon, sliced $\frac{1}{4}$-inch thick,
   seeds removed

1. Marinate the fish in the lime juice, garlic, and parsley for 15 minutes at room temperature.

2. Heat the grill to medium (350°F). Grill fish, about 4 minutes per side for a 1-inch thick fillet. This will produce a medium internal temperature on the fish. If you prefer medium-well to well done, grill another minute or so on each side.

3. While fish is grilling, heat butter in a skillet over medium heat. Peel cucumber and cut in half lengthwise, then crosswise into $\frac{1}{4}$-inch half-moons. Cook slices until tender, about 4 minutes. Season with salt and pepper.

4. To serve, divide cooked cucumber between 4 warmed plates. Top with grilled fish and $\frac{1}{3}$ cup Coriander Sauce. Garnish with lemon slices.

Coriander Sauce:

$\frac{1}{2}$ cup chopped onion
2 cups 2% milk, divided
2 tablespoons arrowroot or cornstarch
2 tablespoons ground coriander
1 sprig fresh thyme
Salt and freshly ground white pepper
   to taste

1. Lightly coat a skillet with nonstick spray and heat over medium heat. Stir in onions and cook until tender, about 3 minutes, stirring occasionally.

2. Whisk $\frac{1}{2}$ cup milk with arrowroot in a small bowl. Set aside.

3. Pour remaining milk into the skillet and stir in coriander and thyme. Bring to a boil slowly over medium heat. Whisk in arrowroot mixture and cook until thickened, just a minute or so.

4. Season with salt and pepper. Strain before serving.

Asian Vegetable Stir-Fry

*T*his dish has it all — color, crunch, flavor — everything but fat. Oh well, you can't have everything. You won't miss the fat, I promise. Notice that I've split the bok choy into the stalks and leaves. The stalks need to cook a couple of minutes more than the leaves do. If you buy about 8 ounces of bok choy you'll have enough to get a cup of each out of it. Make the soy vinaigrette while you prepare the vegetables, as it takes about 25 minutes to prepare.

SERVES 4 TO 6

½ cup Soy Vinaigrette (recipe follows)
1 cup thinly sliced bok choy stalks
1 cup thinly sliced red onion
2 cups peeled, matchstick cut carrots
2 cups thinly sliced shiitake
    mushroom caps

1 cup thinly sliced bok choy leaves
2 cups thinly sliced snow peas
2 cups thinly sliced napa
    (Chinese) cabbage
Freshly ground black pepper

1. Spray a large wok or chef's pan* with nonstick spray and set over medium-high heat.

2. Pour in soy vinaigrette and when it comes to a boil, stir in the vegetables in the order listed, pausing about a minute while stirring before adding the next ingredient. Sauté until vegetables are crisp-tender, about 1 more minute after you add the cabbage. Season with pepper to taste.

Soy Vinaigrette:
(Makes ½ cup)
2 tablespoons rice wine vinegar
¼ cup plus 1 tablespoon low-sodium
    soy sauce
1 tablespoon fresh grated ginger
1 cup plum wine**
2 tablespoons honey

1. Bring vinegar, soy sauce, ginger, and plum wine to a boil in a small saucepan over high heat. Reduce heat to medium-high and gently boil until sauce reduces by half, about 15 to 20 minutes.

2. Strain through cheesecloth or a fine mesh strainer and pour into a clean saucepan. Bring to a boil and stir in honey until dissolved. Remove from heat. May be prepared 2 days in advance. Cool, then store covered in the refrigerator.

A chef's pan is a large pan with a flat bottom and slightly rounded sides. It generally holds 4 to 6 quarts. Sometimes it is called an "everyday" pan.

**Plum wine is very sweet and you'll find it next to the sake on the liquor aisle. If you can't find it, substitute with apple juice.*

Tropical Fruit Crêpes

*T*he best part about this, other than the mellow tropical taste, is that you can make the crêpes far in advance and freeze them. This crêpe batter is lower in fat than traditional crêpes, and therefore won't cook quite the same. They'll look a little rougher, with lace-like browning. The recipe makes about 14 crêpes, but you only need 8 for this recipe. A caramel sauce thinned with apricot nectar bathes the fresh fruit slices, creating a juicy, sweet filling. (See photograph on page P-13.)

<u>SERVES 4</u>

Crêpes:
2 cups 2% milk
1 cup flour
Pinch salt
3 eggs
3 tablespoons butter, melted

Fruit Filling:
¼ cup sugar
1 tablespoon water
½ cup apricot nectar

1 teaspoon butter
1 mango (about 12 ounces) peeled, and thinly sliced
1 papaya (about 12 ounces) peeled and thinly sliced

Garnish:
Whipped cream
Powdered Sugar
Mint

To make crêpes:

1. Place all crêpe ingredients (milk through melted butter) in a blender and purée until smooth. Let batter rest for 30 minutes at room temperature, or overnight in the refrigerator, in an airtight container.

2. Lightly coat a small nonstick pan or crêpe pan with nonstick cooking spray and place over medium-low heat.

3. Swirl a scant ¼ cup (2 ounces) of batter around bottom pan, returning pan to heat to cook. Watch for tiny pinhole bubbles to break on the surface. Flip when edges turn golden brown, about 2 minutes. Shake the pan to loosen the crêpe or use a small spatula.

4. Cook the other side until golden brown, about another minute. Remove crêpe and reheat pan before adding next batter. Re-spray with nonstick spray after every other crêpe, and occasionally stir the batter. Crêpes can be made a day or two in advance, or even 1 month in advance, if frozen. Store each crêpe in between parchment or wax paper and wrap stack of crêpes with plastic wrap before storing in a resealable plastic bag.

To make filling:

1. Stir sugar and water together in a small but tall saucepan. Cook over medium-high heat, without stirring, until sugar is golden brown, about 4 to 6 minutes, swirling the pan toward the end to promote even coloring. Remove from heat.

2. Slowly pour apricot nectar into hot sugar, a little at a time, being careful to avoid the splattering hot liquid.

3. Return pan to heat and cook, stirring constantly, until sugar dissolves into nectar, about 2 minutes. Remove from heat, stir in butter, and cool slightly. You can make the filling up to this point 1 day in advance.

continued on next page

Store covered in the refrigerator. When ready to serve, gently stir in mango and papaya slices.

To serve:

1. Place a crêpe on a dessert plate. Top with 1 tablespoon of sauce and a slice of papaya and mango.

2. Roll up crêpe and drizzle with a little more fruit syrup. Garnish with a dollop of whipped cream. Sprinkle with powdered sugar and add a sprig of mint. Serve 2 crêpes per person.

CARAMELIZING SUGAR

Not long ago, the thought of caramelizing sugar would send shivers up my spine. I was terrified of it, afraid that my sugar would crystallize and I'd never see the crystal-clear, dark amber liquid I so desperately needed. Dramatic? Me? Well, yes. After crystallizing five pans of sugar in a row, I had good reason to fear the process.

Along the way, I've learned two things. One, a few little tricks can help prevent sugar from crystallizing; and two, if you just want caramel to drizzle over your ice cream or apple tart, you can still make a decent sauce even if your sugar does crystallize.

Sugar crystallizes because of impurities either in the sugar or on the pan or utensil used to stir the sugar. Using a well-known brand name sugar and storing it properly will eliminate the first issue. A copper pan is supposed to help prevent crystallization, and I've found that my sugar rarely crystallizes when I use my copper-lined pan. If you don't have a copper pan, you can try one or more of the following tips. I've been known to try a couple of them at the same time. See if one of these will work for you. And go buy that copper sugar pan you've always wanted.

- If your recipe calls for water and sugar (opposed to the dry method of cooking sugar without a liquid), stir the sugar and water together only in the beginning, never after the sugar begins to melt.

- Cover the pan with a lid for the first 2 minutes of cooking. Steam from the water will form condensation on the lid that will wash down the sides of the pan, where a stray crystal of sugar may be clinging from the earlier stirring. It only takes one crystal to ruin a whole pan.

- Instead of covering the pan with a lid, you may choose to brush down the sides of the pan with a clean pastry brush dipped in cold water to remove any stray sugar crystals.

- Add a tiny amount of acid (a couple of drops of lemon juice or a pinch of cream of tartar) to the sugar and water in the beginning while stirring.

- Add a small amount of corn syrup in the beginning, stirring to distribute the syrup among the sugar and water.

Don't be afraid. The worst that can happen is that the sugar crystallizes, forming that opaque, white crusty film on top. If you need crystal clear caramel for flan or crème caramel, you might need to start over and try more than one of the above tips in combination. If you're making a caramel sauce that you are going to add butter and cream to anyway, let the sugar continue to cook. Eventually, the white crust will melt again. Your amber liquid won't be as clear, but after you add the butter and the cream, you won't notice.

One Grand Cypress
Boulevard
Orlando, FL 32836
407.239.1234
www.grandcypress.
hyatt.com

Golf Courses: The New
Course (18), North (9),
South (9), East (9)

Designer: Jack Nicklaus

Available holes: 45

Accommodations:
750 guestrooms,
including suites

Rates: $$–$$$$

Other Activities:
Equestrian Center,
racquet club, water sports,
nature walk

Think of central Florida, and a certain theme park might come to mind. For golfers, something else comes to mind: playing the New Course at Grand Cypress Resort, inspired by the famed St. Andrews Old Course. Practically next door to Walt Disney World®, this 1,500-acre resort easily lives up to the grand part. A massive, T-shaped hotel features an 18-story atrium lush with tropical trees, some reaching more than 30 feet. Just down the road from the hotel, the Villas of Grand Cypress offer 146 spacious club suites situated alongside the golf course.

A striking free form pool complex with water slides, falls, elaborate cave-like structures, and more than 800,000 gallons of water winds around the back of the hotel, like a tropical lagoon. A few steps beyond the pool, brightly colored sailboats dreamily float on Lake Windsong, a 21-acre lake, partially framed by a white sandy beach. Forty-five holes of golf, all designed by the Golden Bear, await any level of golfer. The New Course is 18 holes, while the North, South, and East courses are nine holes each, but integrate to play 18 with the North-South, South-East, or East-North combinations.

Golfers may choose to dine at the clubhouse either at The Club, a casual restaurant and sports bar or the gourmet Black Swan. The hotel offers five dining venues. La Coquina is an exquisite formal dining room featuring cuisine with multi-cultural inspirations. Hemingways, an old Key West-style restaurant specializes in fresh seafood. A 35-foot bronze mermaid sculpture and fountain anchor an impressive all-day dining room, Cascade. The White Horse Saloon and Steakhouse is for beef and free-range chicken lovers, and the Palm Café and General Store offers deli-style fare to go or casual indoor/outdoor seating. The following recipes represent the delectable cuisine from La Coquina.

Dinner Menu:

SHRIMP & SWEET CORN RAVIOLI
WITH CRACKED BLACK PEPPER SAUCE

• SEARED AHI TUNA SALAD
WITH CITRUS COCONUT VINAIGRETTE

• HEARTS OF PALM GRATINÉE

• CHOCOLATE CHARLOTTE
WITH WHIPPED MASCARPONE & MOCHA BROTH

• *Recipe included*

Golf Pro's Tip

Jack Nicklaus designed all the courses. Most of the greens are somewhat elevated and fast. With the fairways cut very low, it's not a bad idea to pull out the "Texas Wedge," which is the putter, when near the green.

Signature Hole

South course, Number 6 — a favorite among tour players, the narrow fairway on this three-shotter par 5 traverses through mounds, pot bunkers, and water. The approach to the high plateau green must be precise.

Seared Ahi Tuna Salad

*P*icture pretty, this dish literally pops off the plate with a symphony of colors and flavors. Resort chefs are able to get different shaped cuts of tuna than us mere mortals, like triangles and squares. You do want to choose the thickest cut you can so that the center of the tuna remains a deep maroon to contrast with the tawny seared edges. Mizuna is a delicate Japanese green with feathery edges and is usually one of the greens in a mixed baby green ensemble often referred to as mesclun mix. Tatsoi is another Asian green, sometimes called rosette bok choy. Plain bok choy is not a good substitute for this peppery green. Try watercress as a substitute if you cannot find tatsoi. Even with the substitutions, this is one of the best recipes in the book. (See photograph on page P-14.)

SERVES 6

6 (6-ounce) ahi tuna steaks
Salt and freshly cracked
  coarse black pepper
2 tablespoons peanut oil
6 cups (4 ounces) mizuna or
  mixed baby greens
2 cups tatsoi or watercress
2 cups radicchio, thinly sliced
½ cup peeled, matchstick cut carrots
½ cup matchstick cut cooked red beets

½ cup matchstick cut daikon*
¾ cup citrus coconut vinaigrette,
  divided (recipe follows)
1 (3-pound) pineapple, peeled, cored,
  and sliced into 18 thin rounds
4 tablespoons sweet Thai
  chile sauce**
⅔ cup chopped glazed
  macadamia nuts***

1. Season tuna steaks with salt and a generous coating of cracked black pepper. Heat a skillet over high heat. When hot, add peanut oil. Working in batches, quickly sear tuna on all sides (including the ends), about 2 to 3 minutes total time. This will produce a rare steak. Remove from pan and cool a couple of minutes. Cover and refrigerate while assembling the salad. May be prepared a couple hours in advance.

2. Toss the mizuna, tatsoi, and radicchio with ½ cup citrus coconut vinaigrette. Drizzle a tablespoon of vinaigrette separately on the carrots, beets, and daikon.

3. Arrange 3 slices of pineapple in the center of a chilled plate. Place a mound of dressed greens on top. Mound greens to add height, and so pineapple slices peek out underneath. Scatter the carrots, beets,

and daikon on the greens and around the plate, distributing evenly between the 6 plates. Drizzle about 1½ teaspoons Thai chile sauce around the rim of each plate.

4. Slice each tuna steak against the grain into ½-inch slices. Fan slices on top of greens. Sprinkle chopped nuts over plate.

Daikon is a white, mild, radish-flavored Asian root that's shaped more like a large, wide carrot than a radish.

**Thai Kitchen® makes a spicy Thai chile sauce that lists sugar as the second ingredient, and even though "sweet" is not part of the title, it is sweet.*

***Mauna Loa makes a butter candy glazed macadamia nut, available in some gourmet shops and on the Internet. Substitute dry-roasted macadamia nuts if you can't find glazed ones.*

Citrus Coconut Vinaigrette

*C*reamy, sweet, and markedly tart at the same time, this juicy dressing starts with a citrus vinegar that's quick and easy to make. It's so delicious, you'll be tempted to drink it.

(MAKES 1 CUP)

Citrus Vinegar:
2 tablespoons sugar
2 tablespoons rice wine vinegar
2 tablespoons orange juice
1 tablespoon lime juice
1 tablespoon lemon juice

2 teaspoons Dijon mustard
1 teaspoon minced shallots
⅛ teaspoon fresh cracked black pepper (coarse grind)
¼ vegetable oil
⅓ cup coconut milk
Salt and freshly ground white pepper

1. Heat sugar and vinegar in a small saucepan over medium heat. Stir until sugar dissolves. Remove from heat and stir in juices. Chill.

2. Pour citrus vinegar into a blender. Add mustard, shallots, and cracked black

pepper. Purée until smooth. Drizzle in the oil with the blender running, then drizzle in coconut milk, blending until smooth.

3. Season with salt and white pepper. May be prepared 2 days in advance. Chill covered.

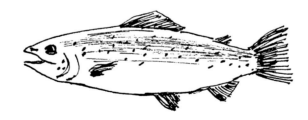

Hearts of Palm Gratinée

*T*t's not likely that you'll find fresh hearts of palm at your market, unless you live in Florida. The Sambal Palmetto (cabbage palm) is the state tree of Florida, and the heart of the tree is what we know as hearts of palm. I made this with canned hearts of palm with good results. Maytag blue is an American blue cheese made in Iowa, and is creamier than Roquetfort or Gorgonzola. See Sources, page 203, for information about how to order it, or check with your specialty grocery store. This dish is very rich, so a little goes a long way. I garnished this with cooked crumbled bacon to add another flavor dimension.

SERVES 6

2 (14-ounce) cans hearts of palm, drained
1 cup heavy cream
6 ounces (about 1 cup) Maytag blue cheese, crumbled

Salt and freshly ground black pepper
1 cup fresh bread crumbs*
3 sliced cooked, crumbled bacon

1. Heat oven to 350°F. Rinse hearts of palm in cold water and drain. Place hearts in a saucepan and pour in cream. Bring to a boil over medium heat. Remove from heat and strain hearts, reserving cream. Cut hearts in half crosswise then cut each piece into quarters.

2. Toss hearts of palm with 6 tablespoons of reserved cream and blue cheese. Season with salt and pepper. Scoop about ½ cup into 6 (6-ounce) custard cups. Season fresh bread crumbs with salt and pepper. Top custard cups with 2 tablespoons of bread crumbs.

3. Bake until hot and bubbly, about 10 minutes. Turn broiler to high and brown tops, about 30 seconds. Remove from oven and cool a couple of minutes before serving. Garnish with crumbled bacon.

* The easiest way to get fresh bread crumbs is to pulse torn bread pieces in a food processor. You need about 3 slices of white bread, crusts removed, to yield 1 cup of crumbs. I chose sourdough bread for this recipe, although white bread would work, too.

Chocolate Charlotte

WITH WHIPPED MASCARPONE & MOCHA BROTH

The name says Charlotte, that quintessential molded French dessert of ladyfingers, Bavarian cream, and fruit, but the flavor is pure tiramisù, with coffee and chocolate flavors accented with chocolate chip-studded mascarpone. Even though there are several components, it isn't hard to do, just a bit time consuming. The Mocha Broth should be made the day before, and the cake, mascarpone, and almond bark can also be prepared 1 day in advance. Every minute of labor pays off in each rich, luscious bite.

SERVES 6

Components (recipes follow):
Vanilla Bean Génoise (cake)
Mocha Broth
Whipped Chocolate Chip
    Mascarpone (filling)
Almond Bark

Whipped cream
Cocoa powder (dusting)

Special equipment:
3-inch cookie cutter
6 (3-inch) dessert molds (or clean,
    empty, 15-ounce vegetable cans)*
Pastry bag with plain round tip

1. Cut 18 rounds from cake (3 per dessert). Line a baking sheet that will fit in the refrigerator with parchment paper or a silicone baking mat.

2. Place the dessert molds (or empty cans, both ends removed) on the baking sheet. Place 1 cake round in the bottom of each mold and drizzle with 1 tablespoon of Mocha Broth.

3. Place mascarpone filling in a pastry bag fitted with a plain round tip. Pipe 2 tablespoons of filling on top of soaked cake round.

4. Top with another cake round. Drizzle with more Mocha Broth and pipe more filling. Do this one more time so that you have 3 layers of soaked cake and 3 layers of mascarpone filling. The dessert should be about 3 inches high.

5. Cover the top of the molds with plastic wrap and refrigerate for at least 1 hour, up to 8 hours.

6. To serve, remove molds from refrigerator. Place a dessert on a chilled dessert plate.

7. Use a long, thin knife dipped in hot water to run around the inside edge of each mold to loosen the dessert. Clean the knife often by dipping in hot water and wiping with a paper towel. Gently lift off the mold.

8. Place a dollop of whipped cream on top of the cake and dust the plate and dessert with cocoa powder. Break off a piece of almond bark and stick in the whipped cream.

A 15-ounce can is slightly less than 3 inches in diameter, so if you use the cans as molds, cut the cake with the can so that the circles are the right size. If you are assembling the desserts just before you serve them, you can skip using a mold altogether, and just stack the layers and serve.

Vanilla Bean Génoise

Génoise is a light, airy, sponge cake with a touch of butter. The key to making it light is whipping in lots of air into the egg base and sweetened meringue, then gently folding in a small amount of starch (in this case, flour and cornstarch). Finally, a teensy drizzle of butter adds just the right amount of fat for richness. I have to confess that I did the folding with my hand, fingers spread like a wide-tooth comb. I think it's easier to blend without losing volume that way. Have all your ingredients measured before you begin, and let the eggs sit at room temperature for about 20 minutes to take the chill off for maximum volume when whipping.

4 tablespoons cornstarch
4 tablespoons flour
½ vanilla bean, split
6 egg yolks, room temperature
  (save 3 of the egg whites)

3 whole eggs, room temperature
1 cup sugar (divided)
3 egg whites, completely free of any
  yolk, room temperature
1 tablespoon butter, melted

1. Heat the oven to 375°F. Line a large baking sheet (12 x 18 x 1) with parchment paper. Spray the paper and sides with nonstick spray. Whisk the cornstarch and flour together in a small bowl. Sift the mixture into another bowl with a fine sieve. Set aside for step 6.

2. Scrape the seeds of the vanilla bean into the mixing bowl of a stand mixer. (Save the vanilla bean to flavor sugar or discard.)

3. Add the yolks, whole eggs, and ½ cup sugar to the vanilla seeds. With the whisk attachment, whip on medium speed for 30 seconds. Stop and scrape the sides and bottom of the bowl. Whip on high speed until the volume increases by two-thirds, about 4 to 5 minutes.

4. In a separate mixing bowl, whip the egg whites until soft peaks begin to form, about 1½ minutes. Slowly and only 1 tablespoon at a time, whip in the remaining ½ cup of sugar. If you do this too fast, you'll lose the volume and have to start over. Be patient.

It will take about 5 more minutes to whip in the sugar. The whites will thicken and turn a shiny, glossy white.

5. Slowly and gently, fold the egg white mixture into the egg yolk mixture, a little at a time, with a rubber spatula or by hand.

6. Gently fold the cornstarch and flour mixture into the egg mixture with as few strokes as possible, but making sure the starch is incorporated. Gently mix in melted butter, with just a few strokes.

7. Pour batter into pan, gently spread it to the edges, and smooth the top. Bake until golden brown, about 10 to 12 minutes. The top will spring back to the touch when done.

8. Remove and cool 5 minutes before removing from pan to a cooling rack. May be made 1 day in advance. After completely cooling, wrap in plastic wrap and store in the refrigerator.

Mocha Broth
Makes 1⅓ cups
1 cup sugar
1 cup water
6 packets of single brew coffee (or 6 tablespoons of regular ground coffee, not instant)
¼ cup Kahlúa® or other coffee-flavored liqueur

1. Bring the sugar, water, and coffee packets to a boil in a saucepan over high heat, gently stirring until the sugar dissolves.

2. Stir in the liqueur and remove from heat. Cool, then cover and let mixture sit for 8 hours at room temperature or overnight in the refrigerator.

3. Strain liquid, discarding coffee packets. May be made 1 week in advance. Store covered in the refrigerator. Stir before using.

Whipped Mascarpone
8 ounces mascarpone
½ cup powdered sugar
1 cup heavy cream
½ cup mini semisweet chocolate chips

1. Beat the mascarpone with the powdered sugar and heavy cream until the mixture is firm, about 1½ minutes with an electric mixer on high speed.

2. Gently fold in the mini chocolate chips with a spatula. May be prepared 1 day in advance. Chill covered.

Almond Bark
¼ cup sliced almonds
6 ounces finely chopped semisweet chocolate

1. Heat oven to 350°F. Spread almonds on a small sheet pan and toast until light golden brown, about 3 to 5 minutes. Remove from oven and cool. Finely chop.

2. While the almonds are toasting, melt the chocolate in a double boiler over simmering water.

3. Stir in chopped almonds when chocolate is completely melted.

4. Line a small baking sheet (that will fit in the freezer) with parchment or wax paper.

5. Spread chocolate mixture very thin (⅛-inch thick) onto paper and chill in freezer 5 minutes, or store in the refrigerator until needed. (See step 8 on page 151.)

THE CLOISTER
Sea Island

100 First Street
Sea Island, GA 31561
800.SEA.ISLAND
www.seaisland.com

Golf Courses: Seaside/
Plantation/Retreat

Designers: Tom Fazio/
Rees Jones/Davis Love III

Available holes: 54

Accommodations:
269 guestrooms,
including suites

Rates: $$$–$$$$

Other Activities: annual
food & wine event,
sport shooting,
horseback riding

Southern grace and charm spill out of every nook and cranny of the historic Cloister Hotel off the southern coast of Georgia, on the 5-mile Sea Island. Accommodations extend beyond the charming rooms in the stucco and tile roof hotel. Oceanfront and near seaside luxury rooms now outnumber the original hotel rooms, and the nearby Lodge, opened in 2001, serves up an additional 40 rooms above a grand clubhouse.

Low country salt marshes and white sandy dunes are interspersed with the resort and upscale housing enclaves on the island — a rare case of planned development harmonizing with the environment. Overhead, floating sea gulls seem suspended in time. The resort certainly moves as if it belongs to an earlier time, with gracious, polite, near invisible staff, big band dances, and caddies waiting to guide you through three remarkable golf courses. More than 75 years of legendary golf and genteel hospitality attract privacy-seeking celebrities, generations of the same families returning year after year, and of course, serious golfers.

Guests have a plethora of dining choices to appease the palate. The formal Cloister Main Dining Room (jackets required), features classics like lobster thermidor, aged filet mignon, and domestic rack of lamb alongside new global dishes such as sautéed shrimp in a red Thai curry sauce and strawberry jalapeño soup on ice. Slightly more casual is the oceanside dining at the Beach Club with an extravagant seafood buffet and wild game options. Meat eaters will enjoy the virile Colt & Alison's Steakhouse at The Lodge and all diners will delight in alfresco dining at The Terrace, where the views almost rival the food.

Breakfast Menu

- CHOCOLATE CHIP & PEANUT BUTTER MUFFINS

- SAUSAGE CHEESE BISCUITS WITH SAUSAGE CREAM GRAVY

- LEMON FRENCH TOAST WITH PERSIMMON SYRUP

Dinner Menu

- GRILLED CHICKEN & VEGETABLE SPRING ROLL
  WITH THAI CHILE DIPPING SAUCE

FAR EAST DUCK BREAST WITH COCONUT CURRY
OR
- SLOW-BRAISED BABY BACK RIBS

- ROASTED CORN & LOBSTER SALAD

- TORTILLA-CRUSTED TENDERLOIN WITH ONION CHILE JUS

- PEACH BEGGAR'S PURSE
WITH BOURBON CRÈME ANGLAISE & CIDER REDUCTION

- *Recipe included*

Golf Pro's Tip

The short game is the key to scoring on Seaside. Chipping and pitching may not always be your best option when your ball lies close to the green on the tight grass of the swells. Try putting instead of using an iron to chip or pitch. You'll find that you're much more consistent in getting your ball close to the hole.

Signature Hole

Seaside course, Number 16, par 5 — wide-open fairway is misleading, especially for bold drives that must cross an angled creek. Forward tees skip the water hazard.

Chocolate Chip Peanut Butter Muffins

*M*y Dad doesn't think chocolate and peanut butter go together, but that's because he's not yet had these muffins. Strong on the peanut flavor, and heavy for their size, these muffins were a big hit with all of my tasters, including me.

MAKES 10 TO 12 MUFFINS

6 tablespoons butter, softened
1 cup brown sugar
2 tablespoons light corn syrup
½ cup creamy peanut butter
1 egg
2 egg yolks
1½ cups flour

1½ teaspoons baking powder
½ teaspoon baking soda
¼ teaspoon salt
½ cup milk
¾ cup chocolate chips
½ cup roasted chopped peanuts

1. Heat oven to 375°F. Beat butter with brown sugar and corn syrup, using an electric mixer, for about 2 minutes. Mixture will look grainy. Beat in peanut butter until smooth, about a minute.

2. Beat in egg and yolks for about a minute. Scrape the sides and bottom of the bowl and beat again for a few seconds.

3. Whisk flour, baking powder, baking soda, and salt together in a large bowl.

4. Alternately fold flour mixture with milk into the butter mixture, being careful not to overmix. Fold in chocolate chips and peanuts.

5. Spray a muffin tin with nonstick spray. Fill each cup about three-quarters full (a scant ⅓ cup or #12 ice cream scoop). Bake for 18 to 20 minutes, until tops are dark golden brown and a toothpick inserted in the center comes out with just a few moist crumbs attached.

Sausage Cheese Biscuits

*I*ncredible! Just when you thought a biscuit couldn't get any better, add some cheese and sausage. The resort tops these with sausage cream gravy (made with pure cream), and then crowns it with a little sautéed fois gras. Mon Dieu!

MAKES 10 BISCUITS

5 tablespoons butter, slightly
    softened
2 teaspoons sugar
1¼ cups flour
1 tablespoon baking powder

¼ teaspoon salt
1 cup grated cheddar cheese
½ cup cooked, drained, and cooled
    pork sausage
½ cup buttermilk

1. Heat oven to 400°F. Beat butter and sugar with a wooden spoon until smooth and creamy.

2. Whisk flour, baking powder, and salt together. Work flour mixture into butter with a fork or your hands until the crumbs are pea-size. Stir in cheese and sausage.

3. Mix in buttermilk with as few strokes as possible. Using a ¼ cup measure (or #30 ice cream scoop) scoop out 10 biscuits and place on a baking sheet lined with parchment paper or a silicone baking mat.

4. Bake until light golden brown, about 12 to 15 minutes.

Lemon French Toast

with Persimmon Syrup

emon is just the right balance for the sweetness in this warm, crunchy toast. Start the Persimmon Syrup before you start the toast, as it takes about 30 minutes to prepare. Cook the toast while the syrup is reducing. The key to perfect French toast is browning it on a griddle or in a skillet, and finishing in a hot oven. That way the center is done without browning the crust too much. Persimmons are in season in the fall. If you want to make the syrup but can't find persimmons, substitute ½ cup of fresh apricots, peaches, or even mangos. Frozen peaches will work in a pinch.

Serves 4

2 eggs
1½ cups heavy cream
3 tablespoons sugar
2 teaspoons lemon zest
1 tablespoon lemon juice
½ teaspoon cinnamon

½ vanilla bean, split, or ½ teaspoon
   vanilla extract
1 loaf day-old French bread (1 pound)
   sliced 1-inch thick
Persimmon Syrup (recipe follows)
Powdered sugar for sprinkling

1. Heat oven to 375°F. Beat eggs with cream and sugar. Stir in zest, juice and cinnamon. Scrape the seeds from the inside of the vanilla bean into the cream mixture and whisk to distribute the seeds. (Save the vanilla bean to flavor sugar or discard.)

2. Dip bread slices into cream mixture and place on a baking pan (with sides) to soak up the cream while the griddle is heating.

3. Heat a griddle or nonstick skillet over medium heat. When hot, brush with butter or spray with nonstick spray.

4. Working in batches, brown toast on one side, about 3 to 4 minutes, then flip and brown the other side an additional 2 to 3 minutes. Repeat with remaining bread.

5. Place an ovenproof cooling rack in the oven and place the bread directly on the rack. Bake for 5 minutes, until outside is crispy and interior is done. To serve, sprinkle with powdered sugar and pass the Persimmon Syrup.

Persimmon Syrup:
(Makes 2¼ cups)
2 (6-ounce) persimmons (see note)
2 cups water
2⅔ cups sugar
1 tablespoon lemon zest

1. Cut persimmons in half. Scoop out flesh. Discard seeds and skin. Purée flesh in a mini-food processor or blender until smooth, stopping to scrape the sides of the bowl with a spatula a couple of times. You should have about ½ cup, give or take a little.

2. Bring water and sugar to a gentle boil.

3. Stir in persimmon purée and cook until mixture reduces by about half, and is thick and syrupy, about 20 to 30 minutes.

4. Remove from heat and stir in lemon zest. May be prepared 1 day in advance. Store covered in the refrigerator for up to 5 days.

NOTE: Hachiya persimmons are more widely available than the fuyu persimmon. Both are red-orange in color, but the fuyu is round, like a tomato while the hachiya is slightly elongated with a pointed end.

Grilled Chicken & Vegetable Spring Roll

*I*f you love fried spring rolls, you might be in for a shock tasting one of these. It's made with a translucent rice paper wrapper that's been rehydrated in water. It tastes fresh, with a soft wrapper and a crisp, crunchy filling. The rice paper is very delicate so be gentle, but wrap the roll as tight as you can. The key is to cut the vegetables evenly, into little matchsticks, about ⅛-inch thick and 3-inches long. Cut the chicken ¼-inch by 3 inches. You might have to search out an Asian food specialty store to find the rice papers. Cellophane noodles are made from mung beans, sometimes called bean threads or saifun. Look for them in the Asian food section of your grocery store. (See photograph on page P-15.)

SERVES 8

2 teaspoons peanut oil
½ cup matchstick cut peeled carrot
½ cup matchstick cut red onion
½ cup matchstick cut red bell pepper
½ cup matchstick cut hothouse cucumber
1 cup loosely packed chopped cilantro (divided)
1 cup (3 ounces) rehydrated cellophane noodles (see package for directions)

Juice of 1 lime (about 2 tablespoons)
1 tablespoon dark sesame oil
1 teaspoon ground coriander
½ teaspoon cayenne
Salt
1 cup (5 ounces) sliced grilled chicken breast
8 clear rice paper wrappers
Thai Chile Dipping Sauce (recipe follows)

1. Heat peanut oil and quickly sauté carrot, onions, bell pepper, cucumber, and ½ cup chopped cilantro for about a minute, stirring constantly. Remove from heat and chill.

2. Toss rehydrated noodles with lime juice, sesame oil, coriander, cayenne, and the remaining ½ cup cilantro. Season with salt.

3. Gently heat 2 cups of water in a skillet over very low heat. Place the chilled sautéed vegetables, grilled chicken strips, and noodle mixture in front of you. Dip 1 rice paper at a time into the warm water until softened, about 30 seconds. Place paper on a work surface. Smooth out any bubbles with your hands. Lay a small amount of vegetables, chicken strips, and noodles lengthwise just below the center of the paper.

4. Fold the bottom half of the paper over the stuffing and gently squish with your fingers to make the wrapping tight. Fold over both sides and "square up" the sides. Begin rolling from the bottom up, keeping the wrapper as tight as possible. Seal with a little more warm water if necessary. Repeat with remaining wrappers.

5. Chill until ready to serve. May be prepared 1 day in advance. Wrap tightly in plastic wrap and store in the refrigerator. To serve, unwrap rolls and cut each roll in half, at an angle. Serve with Thai Chile Dipping Sauce.

NOTE: A fresh mint leaf rolled in each roll along with the other ingredients is a lovely flavor addition.

Thai Chile Dipping Sauce

*T*his spring roll sauce is deceptive. At first it's sweet, then it zaps you with a mighty dose of HOT! You can cut down on the amount of Asian red chili sauce, but what fun is that? I also like to serve a peanut sauce alongside this spicy one to tame the heat, and it's a wonderful flavor combination. Just mix 2 or 3 tablespoons of creamy peanut butter with ¼ to ½ cup of coconut milk and add a tiny splash of soy sauce for a cool, creamy fire extinguisher.

MAKES 1¼ CUPS

2 tablespoons peanut oil
2 tablespoons finely chopped shallots
2 teaspoons minced garlic
2 teaspoons peeled and grated
   fresh ginger
2 tablespoons finely chopped red
   bell pepper
1 tablespoon fresh chopped basil

2 teaspoons minced fresh lemongrass
   or ½ teaspoon lime zest
1 cup vegetable stock
2 to 4 tablespoons Asian red
   chile sauce
2 tablespoons brown sugar
2 tablespoons soy sauce
2 teaspoons cornstarch
2 teaspoons cold water

1. Heat peanut oil in a saucepan over medium-high heat. Stir in shallots, garlic and ginger. Cook 1 minute, stirring constantly. Stir in remaining ingredients (except cornstarch and water). Bring to a boil.

2. Mix cornstarch and water together and stir into boiling liquid. Continue to boil until mixture thickens. Reduce heat and simmer 2 to 3 minutes. Remove from heat and chill. Store covered in the refrigerator, up to 1 week.

Slow-Braised Baby Back Ribs

*S*tart these the night before because they need to sit overnight in a salt brine. The sweet tangy barbecue sauce is a hallmark of the South. The resort serves these as an appetizer, though you could make them the main attraction.

SERVES 4 TO 6

¼ cup kosher salt
2 racks (2 pounds) baby back ribs,
   cut into 4-bone portions
Water

Sauce:
2 cups tomato sauce
2 cups water
1 cup cider vinegar
1¼ cups brown sugar
2 tablespoons dry mustard
¼ cup hot red pepper sauce
1 tablespoon molasses

1. Rub salt on the ribs and place in a container with a lid that will fit in your refrigerator. Cover ribs with water and store in the refrigerator, covered, overnight.

2. Heat oven to 350°F. Remove the ribs from the brine and rinse well under cold running water. Pat dry with paper towels. Place meaty side down in a large roasting pan.

3. Mix all the sauce ingredients together (tomato sauce through molasses). Reserve 2 cups and pour remaining sauce over ribs, completely coating the ribs. Cover with foil and bake for 3 hours, or until the ribs are tender. Carefully remove from braising liquid, cover with foil and keep warm.

4. Strain 1 cup of the braising liquid into a large skillet (you want the large surface area of a skillet to quicken the reduction process) and stir in the reserved 2 cups of sauce. Bring to a boil. Reduce heat to a strong simmer and cook until liquid is thicker, about 15 to 20 minutes, skimming the foam from the edges as necessary. Taste and add more brown sugar and a little cider vinegar if the sauce is too salty. Meanwhile, heat the broiler.

5. Brush ribs with a little of the sauce and brown under the broiler, about 2 to 3 minutes. Pass the rest of the sauce at the table.

Roasted Corn & Lobster Salad

*C*orn and black beans have always made a tasty combination, and sautéed lobster dresses up this substantial salad considerably. I like to grill corn without the husk so that the kernels get brown marks. One ear will grill in about 3 to 4 minutes over a moderate heat (350°F), turning occasionally. If fresh corn isn't an option, you can pan-roast thawed, frozen corn in a dry skillet until lightly brown. This salad makes a flavorful base for the slow-braised ribs on the previous page.

SERVES 4 TO 6

1 tablespoon butter
1 jalapeño, seeded and minced
1 tablespoon fresh grated ginger
1 pound chopped lobster tail meat*
1 ear corn, grilled

1 cup cooked, drained black beans
2 tablespoons finely chopped red
  bell pepper
2 tablespoons chopped cilantro
Salt and freshly ground black pepper

1. Melt butter in a skillet over medium-high heat. Stir in jalapeño, ginger, and lobster meat. Cook, stirring constantly for 3 minutes. Meanwhile, cut corn kernels off cob.

2. Stir corn, black beans, red bell pepper, and cilantro into lobster mixture. Cook, stirring occasionally, until heated through and lobster meat is done, about 1 or 2 minutes. Season with salt and freshly ground black pepper.

*It's easier to remove the tail meat from the shell by parcooking it. Make sure the tail is thawed if it was frozen. Bring 12 to 16 cups of water to a boil in a large pot. Boil lobster tail for about 3 minutes. Remove tail from boiling water and plunge into a large bowl of ice water to stop the cooking. After 5 minutes remove tail from water and cut underside of lobster shell with kitchen scissors. Remove shell and cut the lobster meat into ½-inch cubes. Season with salt and pepper before proceeding to step 1.

Tortilla-Crusted Tenderloin

WITH ONION CHILE JUS

The Cloister uses a venison loin chop for this recipe. I also tried it with a pork chop and with a beef tenderloin filet, so you have lots of options. The only difference is in the cooking times. The venison and beef take about the same amount of time for medium rare, and the pork takes an additional 10 to 15 minutes. The crust is not only delicious, a crunchy corn flavor, but it is also attractive with the mix of blue and white corn chips. The sauce takes about an hour to make, so start the sauce before you start the meat, or make the sauce the day before and gently reheat before serving.

SERVES 6

6 (2-bone) venison chops, about 3
    pounds, or 6 (6-ounce) beef
    tenderloin filets, or 6 (8-ounce)
    boneless double-cut pork chops
2 tablespoons olive oil
Salt and freshly ground black pepper
3 eggs
½ cup Dijon mustard
1 cup crushed blue corn tortilla chips

1 cup crushed white corn tortilla chips

Jus:
3 large sweet onions (about 1½
    pounds), sliced ¼-inch thick
2 tablespoons olive oil
1 to 2 whole pequín dry chiles*
2 cups demi-glace**
Salt and freshly ground black pepper

1. Heat oven to 375°F. Heat a skillet over high heat until hot. Brush meat with olive oil and season with salt and pepper. Sear on all sides until brown, 3 to 4 minutes total. Cool for 5 minutes or so.

2. Beat eggs with mustard. Toss blue and white corn chips together in a separate bowl.

3. Brush cooled meat with egg mixture and roll in tortilla chips. Place coated meat on a baking sheet and roast until internal temperature reaches 125°F. (for medium rare), about 8 to 10 minutes for the venison or beef. For the pork chops, roast until the internal temperature reaches 145°F. for medium, about 18 to 20 minutes.

4. Remove and rest, uncovered, for 5 minutes before serving. Serve with Onion Chile Jus. (The crust will turn soggy from the steam if you cover the meat.)

To make jus:

1. Cook onions slowly in the olive oil over medium heat until caramelized, about 45 to 55 minutes. Stir occasionally in the beginning, and more frequently toward the end to prevent uneven browning or burning. May be prepared up to 3 days in advance, stored covered in the refrigerator. Reheat before proceeding with step 2.

2. Stir chiles into onions and pour in demi-glace. Bring to a boil then reduce to a slow simmer and cook 10 to 15 minutes, allowing the chile flavor to impart. Remove whole chiles before serving. Season with salt and pepper.

*The pequín chile is a tiny dried red chile that hits the heat scale at about 8 or 9 out of 10, meaning it's fiery hot. The longer de árbol chile or a teaspoon of red pepper flakes are good substitutions.

**See Demi-glace under Common Procedures, page 17.

Peach Beggar's Purse

Sometimes I like to make complex desserts. Fortunately, this recipe allows me the opportunity to do so. The delicate, crisp shell contains a delightful surprise inside — a juicy peach half with a dollop of dark chocolate in the center. The accompanying two sauces layer more flavors, including a mellow bourbon vanilla crème and a spicy apple note. You can wrap the peaches early in the day, cover and refrigerate until you're ready to bake. Make the sauces before you start, too, even the day before. I did try this with canned peaches in addition to fresh ones, just in case I wanted to make it out of peach season, and it wasn't nearly as good. (See photograph on page P-24.)

SERVES 8

1 cup heavy cream
1 tablespoon corn syrup
8 ounces semisweet chocolate, chopped
4 small, ripe, fresh peaches (about 1½ pounds)

24 sheets phyllo dough, thawed
1 cup (2 sticks) butter, melted
½ cup sugar
Bourbon Crème Anglaise (recipe follows)
Cider Reduction (recipe follows)

1. Bring the cream and corn syrup to a boil. Remove from heat. Place the chocolate pieces in a large bowl and pour the hot cream over the chocolate. Cover with plastic wrap and let stand 2 to 3 minutes. Stir until all the chocolate is melted and the mixture is smooth. Cool, uncovered, in the refrigerator until thick. You can dip the bowl in ice water to speed up the cooling process.

2. While chocolate is cooling, bring a large pot of water to boil. Prepare a large bowl of ice water. Wash peaches and remove stem. Cut an "X" on the bottom of each peach, not too deep, just through the skin. Gently lower peaches into the boiling water. Cook 2 minutes, remove and drop in ice water to stop the cooking process. Leave peaches in ice water for several minutes, then remove and slip skins off. Cut in half lengthwise, and carefully remove pit, keeping each half intact.

3. Unwrap the thawed phyllo dough, cover with a piece of plastic wrap then a damp kitchen towel. Remove 1 sheet to a work surface and completely cover the remaining sheets to keep them from drying out. Cut the piece into a 12-inch square with a sharp knife. Brush square with melted butter then sprinkle lightly with ½ teaspoon of sugar. Place another phyllo sheet on top and trim off excess with a sharp knife. Butter and sprinkle with sugar. Repeat 1 more time so that you have 3 layers.

4. Place a peach half in the center of the phyllo square. Scoop 2 tablespoons of cooled chocolate into the center. Save remaining chocolate for later.

5. Pull up the sides of the phyllo dough around the peach, creating a drawstring shaped purse. Brush the sides and bottom with more butter as you gather up the sides. Squeeze the dough tightly above the peach to seal in the peach, creating a pretty "flower" of dough above the point you squeezed. Brush the top gently with more melted butter and set on a lined baking sheet.

6. Repeat with remaining phyllo dough and peaches. Gently cover with plastic wrap and refrigerate or if ready to bake, heat oven to 400°F. When oven is hot, bake until golden brown, about 15 to 20 minutes. Cover tops of purses with a square of foil after 5 minutes of baking to prevent over-browning while allowing the sides to brown. Rotate the pan once during baking to promote even browning.

7. Cool slightly. Ladle ¼ cup Bourbon Crème Anglaise on the bottom of a dessert plate. Drizzle 2 tablespoons of Cider Reduction over sauce. Place a phyllo peach in the center and drizzle with the warm leftover chocolate sauce. Beautiful!

Bourbon Crème Anglaise:
(Makes 2 cups)

This sauce cooks fast, so have all your ingredients and tools ready, especially a bowl of ice water to chill the sauce after cooking. Like any cold sauce made with eggs, it's important to keep this sauce chilled until ready to serve. You can make this a day or two in advance, but don't keep it more than 3 days total, and always keep it cold. Now that I've scared you, relax and think about how creamy and delicious this is, with an appreciable bourbon flavor. You'll be tempted to pour a glass.

2 vanilla beans
1¼ cups heavy cream
4 tablespoons bourbon
3 tablespoons sugar
7 egg yolks

1. Fill a large bowl with ice water and set aside. Split vanilla beans and scrape seeds with a sharp knife into a saucepan. (Save beans for flavoring sugar or discard). Pour in cream and bourbon. Whisk in sugar. Bring mixture just to a boil over medium heat, whisking occasionally. Remove from heat.

2. Beat the egg yolks in a small bowl, then slowly add a little of the hot cream to the eggs, stirring constantly to prevent eggs from cooking. Stir in a little more cream, continuing to add and stir in more cream to warm the eggs. Pour warmed eggs back into the rest of the cream mixture and place pan over medium-low heat, stirring often, until mixture thickens, about 1 to 3 minutes.

3. Strain the sauce into a bowl and set that bowl in the large bowl of ice water. Stir occasionally until chilled. May be made 1 day in advance. Stored covered in the refrigerator.

Cider Reduction:
(Makes 1 cup)

In addition to adding a spicy layer to the peach dessert, this sauce perfumes your house while it cooks.

1 vanilla bean, split
1½ cups apple cider or juice
⅔ cup apple brandy (like Applejack)
⅓ cup sugar
4 cinnamon sticks, or ¼ teaspoon cinnamon
4 whole cloves, or pinch ground cloves
4 whole black peppercorns

1. Scrape vanilla bean seeds into a saucepan with a sharp knife. (Save the vanilla bean for flavoring sugar or discard.) Stir remaining ingredients into the saucepan and bring to a boil over high heat, stirring once or twice. CAUTION: brandy is extremely flammable. Remove pan from heat before adding brandy and use care when heating any alcohol.

2. Gently boil the sauce until it reduces by half, about 15 minutes. Strain and cool. May be made 1 to 3 days in advance. Store covered in the refrigerator.

PINEHURST.
1895

A Pinehurst Company Resort

1 Carolina Vista Dr.
Village of Pinehurst,
NC 28374
800.487.4653
www.pinehurst.com

Golf Courses:
Eight courses, simply
named by number,
including famed No. 2

Designers: Donald Ross/
Dan Maples/Rees Jones/
Tom Fazio

Available holes: 144

Accommodations:
520 guestrooms,
including suites

Rates: $–$$$
Modified American Plan

Other Activities:
Spa, tennis,
croquet, swimming,
village shopping

Three things are sacred in North Carolina: NASCAR, college basketball, and Pinehurst golf. Located 65 miles southeast of Raleigh, in the south central part of the state called the "Sandhills," Pinehurst sits on 2,000 acres and is a golf mecca for amateurs and professionals alike. More tournament golf is played at Pinehurst than any other location.

While the No. 2 course is perhaps the most widely recognized, the Fazio redesigned No. 4 is high on returning guests' list of courses to play, as is No. 7. The prettiest course is No. 5, especially noted for the 15th hole, known as the "Cathedral," with a picturesque pond in front of the green, dotted with dogwoods, and framed by old pines that resemble organ pipes; hence, the name.

Pinehurst is the perfect place for the half-golf couple. You know the one that fanatically loves golf and the other one doesn't? The Village of Pinehurst (walking distance from the hotel) offers an abundant collection of quaint cottage shops and restaurants, tucked among pine trees and hardwoods, along cobblestone streets. The new, sparkling 31,000-square-foot Pinehurst Spa can keep the non-golfer occupied for days, while the golf lover lives the dream of playing courses that have hosted the most revered golfers throughout time.

The food is just as soul-satisfying as the golf. Dining at the resort runs the gamut from classic Southern in the Carolina Dining Room and the upscale 1895 Room, to an authentic re-creation of a 19th century Scottish pub called The Tavern, to several casual grills, including the Donald Ross and Mulligan's.

Breakfast Menu

- Carrot Spice Miniature Muffins

- Prosciutto & Romano Cheese Grits

- Sweet Potato Biscuits

Dinner Menu

- Chilled Crab Tower with Lemon Crème Fraîche

- Chilled Peach Bisque

Grilled Double-Bone Lamb Chop & Seared Veal Medallion with Huckleberry Gastrique

Root Vegetable & French Bean Medley

Russet & Sweet Potato Rösti

- Chocolate Amaretto Terrine with Fresh Berry Coulis

- Double Chocolate Indulgence Cookies

- *Recipe included*

Golf Pro's Tip

Eight courses test every part of your game. Watch out for more than 170 pot bunkers on No. 4 and undulating greens of the famous No. 2 golf course.

Signature Hole

Actually, it's an entire course, No. 2 — with a complete package of distance, strategic bunkers, menacing water features, and brutishly undulating greens.

Carrot Spice Miniature Muffins

*A*lthough the flavor is similar to a carrot cake, these muffins are not even close to being that sweet, which makes them perfect for breakfast and brunch. I also like to serve them at lunch with a light chicken salad. If you make regular muffins instead of the mini ones, increase the baking time by a few minutes.

Makes 54 miniature muffins or 18 regular muffins

3½ cups cake flour
1½ cups sugar
2 teaspoons cinnamon
1½ teaspoons baking soda
½ teaspoon salt
4 eggs
1 cup vegetable oil

1 teaspoon vanilla extract
2 cups grated carrots
    (about ¾ pound)
1 apple, peeled, cored, and grated
⅔ cup coconut
¼ cup raisins
½ cup finely chopped pecans

1. Heat oven to 400°F. Whisk first 5 ingredients (cake flour through salt) together in a large bowl.

2. Beat eggs with oil and vanilla in a separate bowl. Stir carrots, apple, coconut, and raisins into egg mixture.

3. Pour carrot mixture over flour mixture and stir just to moisten, folding in pecans at the end. A few small lumps are fine.

4. Spray muffin tins with nonstick spray and fill each tin three-quarters full, about 2 tablespoons (a #50 ice cream scoop works great). Bake until a toothpick inserted in the center comes out clean, about 11 to 13 minutes.

5. Remove from oven and cool 1 minute before releasing from pan. Serve warm or at room temperature. Store in an airtight container in the refrigerator for up to 3 days.

Prosciutto & Romano Cheese Grits

M ost American Romano-style cheeses are made from cow's milk. But while in Rome, as they say, do as the Romans do, and seek out an Italian Romano made with tangy sheep's milk. The salt from the cheese combined with briny prosciutto adds up to a fairly salty dish, although the flavor is marvelous. Serve with a dry, sourdough toast to counterbalance the salt. A little of these grits go a long way. Make it a sideshow, not the main attraction, but do make it. It's delicious.

Serves 6

3 cups chicken stock
¾ cup coarse-ground grits
½ cup heavy cream
1 cup grated Romano cheese
1 teaspoon olive oil
1 tablespoon minced shallots

1 teaspoon minced garlic
¼ pound thinly sliced prosciutto, chopped
1 tablespoon fresh thyme leaves
Freshly ground white pepper

1. Bring the chicken stock to a boil in a saucepan. Whisk in the grits and cream until smooth, then turn the heat to low and cover. Cook, stirring occasionally, until all the liquid is absorbed and grits are creamy, 10 minutes or less. Stir in cheese. Keep warm.

2. Heat olive oil in a skillet over medium heat. Add shallots and garlic. Cook, stirring once, until shallots are soft, about a minute. Mix in prosciutto and thyme. Stir mixture into hot grits. Season with freshly ground white pepper.

Sweet Potato Biscuits

*B*iscuits should be in quotation marks. The texture is more like a scone. Spicy with cinnamon and ginger, these warm treats disappeared quickly among my ravenous tasters.

MAKES 12 TO 15 BISCUITS

2½ cups flour
⅓ cup brown sugar
4½ teaspoons baking powder
1 teaspoon cinnamon
½ teaspoon salt
¼ teaspoon ground allspice
⅛ teaspoon ground ginger

⅔ cup shortening, cut into
    small pieces
1½ cups (about 1 pound) cooked,
    mashed sweet potatoes
⅔ cup chopped toasted pecans*
½ cup heavy cream

1. Heat oven to 400°F. Whisk first 7 ingredients (flour through ginger) together in a large bowl.

2. Work in shortening with a pastry cutter or your hands until crumbs are pea-size.

3. Stir in sweet potatoes and pecans until barely mixed.

4. Slowly add in heavy cream, a little at a time, allowing cream to incorporate. Try not to overmix (which can make biscuits tough). Dough will be sticky.

5. Transfer dough to a cold surface lightly dusted with flour. Using floured hands, pat the dough into a circle about 10 inches in diameter and ½-inch thick. Cut out 2½-inch circles with biscuit or cookie cutters. Turn cut biscuits upside down so the bottom is now facing up on an ungreased baking sheet. (This helps the biscuits rise a little higher, although because of the sweet potatoes, they will be flatter than regular biscuits.)

6. Pat the scraps together and cut out a few more biscuits. Bake until biscuits are golden brown, about 20 to 25 minutes. Serve warm with butter.

*To toast nuts, see page 18 under Common Procedures.

Chilled Blue Crab Tower

WITH LEMON CRÈME FRAÎCHE

*T*owers of food, if done tastefully, are still in style. This dish is stunning, but the best part is the fresh taste, especially if you splurge on the crabmeat and buy only the best. Blue crab is easy to find along the East Coast and the Gulf of Mexico near Florida, but other lump crabmeat will work in this dish, too, such as Dungeness. Please promise me you won't use that canned stuff on the grocery shelf near the canned tuna. Any specialty grocery store or butcher shop will have access to top quality crab, and I've even discovered a quality brand of canned pasteurized crab called Phillips. It's sold through some of the large price warehouse clubs, such as Costco. (See photograph on page P-16.)

SERVES 4

½ pound cooked lump crabmeat
¼ cup olive oil
Zest of 1 lemon
¼ cup fresh chopped mint
Salt and freshly ground black pepper
1 cup (6 ounces) yellow tomatoes,
    peeled, seeded, and chopped
1 (7-ounce) avocado,
    peeled and chopped
1 teaspoon lemon juice
¾ cup finely chopped sweet onion
½ cup spicy sprouts (such as radish)

4 molds*

Garnish:
4 slices sourdough bread,
    ½-inch thick
1 tablespoon butter
Freshly ground black pepper
Lemon Crème Fraîche
    (recipe follows)
Zest of 1 lemon
    (zest at the last minute)
4 mint springs

1. Mix crabmeat with olive oil, lemon zest, and chopped mint. Season with salt and pepper.

2. Season the chopped tomato with salt and pepper to taste. Sprinkle the chopped avocado with the lemon juice and gently toss.

3. Line a baking sheet with parchment paper or plastic wrap. Spray the molds with nonstick spray and place on the lined sheet. Layer the ingredients in this order, packing each layer tight with the back of a spoon and ending with the sprouts:
• 2 tablespoons tomato
• 2 tablespoons crabmeat
• 2 tablespoons avocado

• 1 tablespoon sweet onion
• 2 tablespoons crabmeat
• 2 tablespoons sprouts

4. Cover and refrigerate until ready to serve. May be prepared up to 8 hours in advance.

5. Cut the sourdough slices into decorative shapes with a cookie cutter (the resort uses a crescent-shaped cutter, and I use a star). Brush cut bread with melted butter and sprinkle with freshly ground black pepper. Toast until golden brown. May be prepared 1 day in advance. Store at room temperature in an airtight container.

continued on next page

6. To serve, place a crab mold in the center of a chilled plate. Carefully remove the mold, running a thin knife blade along the inside of the mold to loosen, if necessary. Place a dollop of Lemon Crème Fraîche next to the tower, or place in a squeeze bottle and zigzag on the plate. Garnish with toasted sourdough, freshly ground black pepper, a pinch of lemon zest, and a sprig of mint.

*The resort uses 3 x 3-inch PVC pipes as molds. The Chocolate Charlotte recipe on page 151 also uses 3-inch molds. You could use tomato sauce cans (8-ounce size), both ends removed, washed, and dried for this recipe. The tomato sauce cans aren't quite 3 inches across, but they're close enough.

Lemon Crème Fraîche

There's nothing quite like a homemade crème fraîche, though you could fake it with sour cream thinned with a splash of cream.

MAKES 1 ½ CUPS

1 cup heavy cream
3 tablespoons buttermilk

3 lemons

1. Stir cream and buttermilk together in a clean bowl or sanitized jar. Cover bowl or close jar and allow mixture to sit at room temperature until thickened. This could take anywhere from 12 to 24 hours, depending upon how warm you kitchen is.

2. After mixture is thickened, zest 3 lemons and finely chop the zest. Stir into crème fraîche and refrigerate, covered, until chilled. Store covered in the refrigerator, up to 1 week.

The Homestead Resort, Virginia

Macadamia Nut-Crusted Chicken with Spinach Spätzle

The Greenbrier

Smoked Salmon & Shrimp Tower with Dill Cream & Chile Lime Baby Greens

The Sagamore

Oatmeal Brûlée

The Lodge at Pebble Beach

Golf Links
7th Hole

The Broadmoor

East & West Courses

The Lodge at Koele

Experience at Koele
17th Hole

The Cloister at Sea Island

Plantation Course

Manele Bay Hotel

Challenge at Manele · 12th Hole

The Phoenician

Desert Course
9th Hole

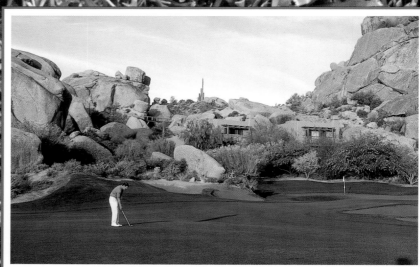

*Hyatt Regency
Grand Cypress*

*North Course
2nd Hole*

The Boulders

*South Course
5th Hole*

Pinehurst

*No. 2 Course
17th Hole*

The Greenbrier

Greenbrier Course
10th Hole

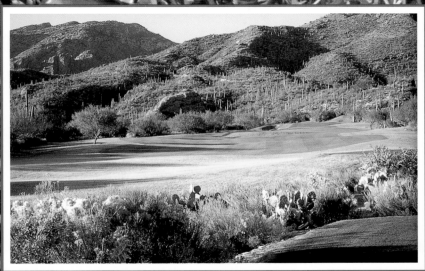

Ventana Canyon
Golf & Racquet Club

Mountain Course
2nd Hole

Doral Golf
Resort & Spa

Blue Monster Course
18th Hole

The Cloister

Peach Beggar's Purse
with Bourbon Crème Anglaise & Cider
Reduction

The Sagamore

1st Hole

The Homestead

Cascades Course
16th Hole

Chilled Peach Bisque

*R*efreshing, not too sweet, with subtle citrus undertones, this is soup delightful, especially during a sunset meal alfresco. Every taster raved about this delicate soup, even Rosalie, my most discriminating taster. This is a good candidate for that special cinnamon I described on page 72.

SERVES 8

3 pounds frozen peaches, thawed
1¼ cups plain yogurt
¾ cup orange juice
¼ cup lemon juice

2 tablespoons sugar
2 tablespoons peach schnapps
  (optional)
1 teaspoon cinnamon

1. Working in batches, purée peaches in a blender until smooth and pour into a large bowl.

2. Whisk in the remaining ingredients until smooth. Taste and add more sugar or schnapps if you'd like. Chill until ready to serve. Store covered in the refrigerator, up to 3 days.

Chocolate Amaretto Terrine

WITH FRESH BERRY COULIS

*J*f you're not a committed chocolate lover, you might want to skip this recipe, because as with many of life's sweetest rewards, it requires a bit of work. The good news is that it makes two loaf pans, and it freezes beautifully. In fact, I like it better frozen. No, I like it chilled. No, I like it...any which way. It's heavenly creamy, rich, and deeply chocolate. I'm committed.

SERVES 16

11 ounces semisweet chocolate, chopped
5 ounces unsweetened chocolate, chopped
2 eggs, separated
2 tablespoons sugar
3 cups heavy cream
4 tablespoons (½ stick) butter

2 tablespoons (1 ounce) almond paste, crumbled
2 tablespoons Amaretto or other almond-flavored liqueur
2 tablespoons rum
2 tablespoons crème de cacao

Garnish:
Fresh mixed berries
Fresh Berry Coulis (recipe follows)

1. Line 2 medium (8½ x 4¼ x 2½) loaf pans with plastic wrap. Fill with hot water for 2 minutes, then drain. This removes any air bubbles. Blot with a paper towel to dry and set aside until ready to use.

2. Melt both chocolates in a double boiler over simmering water.

3. While chocolate is melting, beat the egg whites until soft peaks form, about 1½ to 2 minutes with an electric mixer on high speed. Beat in the 2 tablespoons of sugar. Beat until stiff peaks form, about another minute. Set aside.

4. Whip cream until thick, about 2½ to 3 minutes with an electric mixer on high speed. Keep in refrigerator until step 7.

5. Melt the butter in a small saucepan over medium heat and stir in the almond paste, whisking until smooth (which could take a couple of minutes). Whisk this mixture into the melted chocolate. The mixture will go from smooth to dark and grainy. Mix in the Amaretto, rum, and crème de cacao.

6. Whisk egg yolks in a small bowl. Stir 2 tablespoons of the hot chocolate mixture into the yolks to warm them before whisking the yolks back into the chocolate mixture.

7. Beat a few tablespoons of the whipped cream into the chocolate mixture to smooth. Scrape the chocolate mixture into a large bowl.

8. Gently fold the egg whites, in 2 or 3 stages, into the chocolate mixture, followed by the rest of the whipped cream in 2 or 3 stages.

9. Pour the mixture evenly between the loaf pans. Cover and chill for at least 3 hours. May be made 1 day in advance, and it freezes for up to 1 month. To serve, dip the loaf pan in a large pan of hot water. Place a plate upside down over the top of the loaf pan. Turn the pan over and remove the loaf pan and the plastic wrap. Cut into ½-inch slices to serve.

10. Garnish the plate with fresh berries and Fresh Berry Coulis.

**Fresh Berry Coulis:
(Makes 1 cup)**

This is one of the best berry sauces I've tried, and probably the first one with both white wine and Kirsch, a cherry-flavored clear brandy. Keep it in a squeeze bottle and decorate all your dessert plates that berries would complement.

1 cup mixed fresh or frozen berries
¼ cup white wine
2 tablespoons honey
2 teaspoons Kirschwasser
(cherry brandy)

1. Purée all ingredients in a blender until smooth.

2. Push through a fine sieve to remove seeds.

3. Chill until needed. Store covered in the refrigerator, up to 4 days.

Double Chocolate Indulgence Cookies

J told one of my tasters that these were "to die for," and she said no, these were "to live for." I love positive people! Anyway you look at it these cookies are worth every bite.

MAKES 50 (2-INCH) COOKIES

11 ounces semisweet chocolate, chopped
3 tablespoons butter
3 eggs
1 cup sugar
1 teaspoon instant espresso or coffee powder

1 teaspoon vanilla extract
⅓ cup plus 2 tablespoons cake flour
1 teaspoon baking powder
¼ teaspoon salt
1¼ cups white chocolate chips
½ cup chopped macadamia nuts

1. Heat oven to 400°F. Melt chocolate and butter together in a double boiler over simmering water.

2. Whip eggs until light and frothy, about a minute with an electric mixer. Whisk in sugar, espresso powder, and vanilla.

3. Remove melted chocolate from heat. Stir a few tablespoons of the melted chocolate into the eggs to warm the mixture. Stir the warmed egg mixture back into the chocolate and beat until smooth, about 1 minute.

4. Whisk the cake flour with the baking powder and salt. Stir this mixture into the chocolate mixture and fold in the white chocolate chips and nuts.

5. Drop by rounded teaspoons (a #70 ice cream scoop works great) onto a baking sheet lined with parchment paper or a silicone mate. Bake until edges are dry, about 8 to 9 minutes. These can quickly burn on the bottom, so watch carefully. Remove from oven and cool 1 minute or so before moving to a rack with a spatula to cool completely. Store in an airtight container for up to 1 week.

THE HOMESTEAD® 1766

U. S. Route 220
Main Street
Hot Springs, VA 24445
800.838.1766
www.thehomestead.com

Golf Courses: The Old Course/ Cascades/ Lower Cascades

Designers: Donald Ross/ William Flynn/ Robert Trent Jones, Sr.

Available holes: 54

Accommodations: 506 guestrooms, including suites

Rates: $–$$$ Modified American Plan

Other Activities: Spa, tennis, horseback riding, fly-fishing, mountain hiking & biking

History runs deep at this red brick Georgian-style Southern resort tucked away in the Allegheny Mountains of northwestern Virginia. A classic destination resort (the closest airport is in Roanoke, about 75 miles down the road), the Homestead lures golfers seeking to escape harried city life and indulge in a slow, genteel vacation. Founded in 1766, the Homestead introduced golf 126 years later, with the 1892 opening of six holes. Famed golf architect Donald Ross expanded the Old Course to 18 holes in 1913.

Today's golfers are just as interested in playing the award-winning Cascades course that winds through mountainous terrain. Fast greens and breathtaking waterfalls throughout the course have positioned Cascades as one of the top five resort courses by the leading golf magazines. The Lower Cascades course, the newest of the three, opened in 1963. Large greens and ample fairways beside the rippling Cascades Stream provide a beautiful setting and a slightly misleading sense of ease. Those large greens have some severe contours with strategically placed bunkers providing ample challenges in this peaceful valley floor setting.

Just as challenging is picking a dining spot from among the resort's choices. The traditional formal Dining Room is an experience in regal dining with classically prepared continental cuisine and true to Old South form, requires jackets and ties for gentlemen. The formal 1766 Grille specializes in old-world tableside preparations of classic French and American specialties. The Casino Club, adjacent to the first tee of the Old Course, is a relaxed setting serving hearty American food. Private dining is also available, known as room service in other resorts, but elevated to an aristocratic level by expertly trained staff at the Homestead. Any choice is the right choice, as the cuisine, service, and ambience in each are truly first-class.

Breakfast Menu

- SOUR CREAM RAISIN TEA LOAF

COUNTRY HAM OMELET

- BUTTERMILK BISCUITS

Dinner Menu

CELERY BROTH

- MACADAMIA NUT-CRUSTED CHICKEN
  WITH LEMON CREAM SAUCE

- SPINACH SPÄTZLE

OLD-FASHIONED SPICE CAKE

- *Recipe included*

Golf Pro's Tip

The Homestead's golf is like fine dining at its best. The Cascades is the meat, the Lower Cascades is the potatoes, and the Old Course is dessert. Drive the ball straight and you won't end up in the soup.

Signature Hole

Cascades course, Number 16 — this dogleg-right par 5 is best played with a lay up shot as a pond protects the front of the green. If you decide "to go for the green," beware that it runs downhill toward that beautiful pond.

Sour Cream Raisin Tea Loaf

*T*ender, light, and only slightly sweet, this is a perfect afternoon pick-me-up to go with a cup of tea. Mine didn't make it past breakfast, but I'm guessing it would be perfect for an afternoon tea. I prefer golden raisins to the regular dark raisins (which look like dead bugs, but that's just me). Dried cranberries or cherries would work just as well as raisins.

MAKES 2 MEDIUM LOAVES

12 tablespoons (1½ sticks) butter,
   softened
¾ cup sugar
½ cup sour cream
1 teaspoon vanilla extract
3 eggs

1 cup milk, divided
2 cups flour
2 tablespoons baking powder
⅔ teaspoon salt
1 cup raisins
Powdered sugar for dusting

1. Heat the oven to 325°F. Beat the butter with the sugar until light and fluffy, about 3 minutes with an electric hand mixer.

2. Beat in the sour cream and vanilla. Beat in the eggs, one at a time. Beat in ½ cup of the milk.

3. Whisk the flour, baking powder and salt together. Stir flour mixture into sour cream mixture and mix until almost incorporated. Stir in the rest of the milk. Fold in the raisins. The batter will look a little grainy.

4. Spray 2 medium (8½ x 4½ x 2½) loaf pans with nonstick spray. Divide batter evenly between the pans and bake in the center of the oven until the loaves have pulled away from the edges of the pan and the tops are golden brown, about 50 to 55 minutes. Rotate the pans half way through baking for even browning. A toothpick inserted in the center should come out mostly clean.

5. Remove pans from oven and cool 5 minutes before removing from pans. Cool completely on a wire rack. Dust with powdered sugar before slicing.

Buttermilk Biscuits

I tested several buttermilk biscuit recipes for this book, and these, by far, are the best. Tender inside, golden and crunchy on the outside, it's hard to find a better biscuit. I tested dropping them by ¼ cupfuls, and though they weren't pretty, they had a little more crunch to the crust. My husband's partner, Dave, liked the dropped biscuits better. It's certainly quicker to just drop the dough and bake.

MAKES 14 (2½-INCH) BISCUITS

⅓ cup shortening
1 tablespoon sugar
2 cups flour
2 teaspoons baking powder

1½ teaspoons salt
¼ teaspoon cream of tartar
1 cup buttermilk
½ teaspoon baking soda

1. Heat the oven to 425°F. Beat the shortening and the sugar with a wooden spoon until creamy, about 1 minute.

2. Whisk the flour, baking powder, salt, and cream of tartar together. Work the flour mixture into the butter mixture with your hands until the crumbs are pea-size.

3. Mix the buttermilk with the baking soda and stir into the crumb mixture using a fork until just blended.

4. Lightly dust a large cutting board with flour and scrape the dough onto the board.

5. Pat the dough out to a ¾-inch thick circle. Cut out 14 biscuits with a 2½-inch cookie cutter. Place on an ungreased baking sheet close together, but not touching (about ½-inch apart).

6. Bake in the center of the oven until the tops are lightly brown, about 10 to 12 minutes. Serve hot.

Macadamia Nut-Crusted Chicken

*T*he Homestead makes gorgeous roulades with this recipe, pounding the chicken breasts thin and rolling with a stuffing of wild rice, spinach, sun-dried tomatoes, mushrooms, and about 10 other ingredients before coating with the nut crust. It's such an eye-catching dish. I've presented just the breast, the nut coating, and the sauce for a quick and easy rendition. The tartness of the lemon sauce plays off the richness of the macadamia nut crust like a violin. (See photograph on page P-17.)

SERVES 6

1 cup flour
2 teaspoons salt
1 teaspoon freshly ground
 white pepper
3 eggs, beaten
2 cups dry bread crumbs
 (Japanese panko preferred*)

1 cup ground macadamia nuts
6 (7-ounce) skinned, boned chicken
 breast halves
½ cup peanut oil

Lemon Cream Sauce (recipe follows)
3 tablespoons chopped fresh chives
 or parsley

1. Heat the oven to 350°F. Create 3 bowls for breading. Season the flour with salt and white pepper and place in 1 bowl. Place the beaten eggs in a second bowl. Toss the bread crumbs and ground macadamia nuts in a third bowl.

2. Dip 1 chicken breast in the seasoned flour. Dip floured breast in the egg bowl, turning to coat both sides, and then drop into the bread crumbs. Roll breast in the bread crumbs to coat, patting crumbs into the chicken. Place on a baking sheet and repeat with each breast. May be prepared up to 4 hours in advance. Cover and chill until ready to fry.

3. Heat ½ cup of peanut oil in a deep-sided skillet or cast iron skillet over medium-high heat. When very hot but not smoking, add 2 or 3 chicken breasts, being careful not to overcrowd the pan, and brown evenly on both sides, about 1½ to 2 minutes per side. Remove chicken from oil with tongs and place on a baking sheet. Repeat with remaining breasts. Finish cooking chicken in the oven for 12 to 15 minutes. Remove and let rest, uncovered, for 5 minutes. Slice each breast, at an angle, into ½-inch thick slices.

4. Arrange chicken slices in a fan shape on warm plates. Ladle Lemon Sauce around chicken and sprinkle with chives or parsley.

*Panko is unseasoned Japanese bread crumbs, coarser and flakier than American bread crumbs, and is found on the Asian food aisle of most grocery stores.

continued on next page

Lemon Cream Sauce:
(Makes ¾ cup)
½ cup dry white wine
1 teaspoon minced shallots
½ teaspoon lemon zest
¼ cup lemon juice (from 2 lemons)
1 cup heavy cream
Salt and freshly ground
    white pepper

1. Reduce wine and shallots in a small skillet over medium-high heat until only 2 tablespoons remain, about 8 to 10 minutes.

2. Stir in zest and lemon juice and bring to a strong simmer.

3. Whisk in heavy cream, reduce heat to medium, and simmer for 20 minutes, until thick and creamy. Season with salt and white pepper.

Spinach Spätzle

*B*right green and a striking contrast to the lemony chicken; this German staple is a refreshing change from potatoes or rice. It's fun to make spätzle, and I even purchased an inexpensive spätzle maker that sits on top of the stockpot. This makes dropping the dough into boiling water an easy task. You can make the spätzle a day or two before, dry flat on a baking sheet, and then transfer to a plastic bag to store in the refrigerator. All that's left to do is brown the spätzle in a little butter before serving. (See photograph on page P-17.)

SERVES 8

6 cups water
1 tablespoon salt
8 ounces (10 snugly packed cups)
   spinach, washed and trimmed

4 cups flour
1 teaspoon salt
⅛ teaspoon ground nutmeg
⅛ teaspoon freshly ground
   white pepper
5 eggs
¾ cup warm (not hot) milk

2 tablespoons butter, divided
Salt and freshly ground
   black pepper

1. Prepare a large bowl of ice water. Bring 6 cups of water and 1 tablespoon of salt to a boil. Working in 2 batches, dunk spinach in boiling water for 1 minute. Scoop out spinach with a slotted spoon and dunk into the ice water. Drain and squeeze excess moisture from spinach with your hands, saving liquid.

2. Purée spinach in a blender until smooth and the consistency of ketchup, adding as much of the reserved liquid as necessary to purée. You may have to stop the blender and stir a few times to get the mixture to blend. You should have about ¾ cup of purée when finished. Set aside.

3. Whisk the flour, salt, nutmeg, and white pepper together in a large bowl.

4. Beat the eggs, one at a time, into the warm milk. Stir in the spinach purée.

5. Create a well in the center of the flour mixture. Pour in the spinach mixture and beat with a wooden spoon until smooth. Continue to beat the dough for 30 to 40 more strokes, until a few small air holes break around the edges. The dough will look like green goo, very loose and sticky.

6. Bring a large pot of salted water to a boil. Using a spätzle maker or colander with large holes, scoop a handful of dough and force it through the holes, letting the dough drop into the boiling water. Cook until done, about 1 minute (dough will float on surface). Remove with a slotted spoon and transfer to a bowl of ice water to chill.

7. Drain and dry by spreading dough in a single layer on a baking sheet lined with paper towels. May be made 1 or 2 days in advance. Dry completely and transfer to a plastic bag. Drizzle in a teaspoon or so of olive oil to keep the dough from sticking together. Store in the refrigerator.

8. Working in 2 batches, melt 1 tablespoon of the butter in a large skillet over medium heat. When hot, stir in half the spätzle and cook until lightly brown, about 5 to 8 minutes. Taste and season with salt and pepper. Repeat with the remaining butter and spätzle.

THE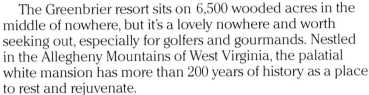

300 West Main Street
White Sulphur Springs,
WV 24986
800.624.6070
www.greenbrier.com

Golf Courses: Old
White/ Greenbrier/
Meadows

Designers: C.B.
MacDonald/Jack
Nicklaus/Robert Cupp

Available holes:
54 holes

Accommodations:
739 guestrooms,
including suites

Rates: $$–$$$$
Modified American Plan

Other Activities:
Spa, tennis, swimming,
fishing, sport shooting,
horseback riding

The Greenbrier resort sits on 6,500 wooded acres in the middle of nowhere, but it's a lovely nowhere and worth seeking out, especially for golfers and gourmands. Nestled in the Allegheny Mountains of West Virginia, the palatial white mansion has more than 200 years of history as a place to rest and rejuvenate.

From meager beginnings as a place to take in healing mineral waters to many roles later, including a Confederate military headquarters during the Civil War, and an army hospital during World War II, The Greenbrier is now known as one of the leading resorts in America. It consistently ranks as the number one resort among discerning travelers.

The traditional Southern resort attracts all types of visitors, including golfers who praise its three championship courses. The Old White course, built in 1913, includes several holes modeled after the most famous European holes. In 1977, Jack Nicklaus redesigned the Greenbrier course, originally opened in 1924. The Meadows course opened in 1999, as a complete redesign of the old Lakeside course.

The Greenbrier is also a center for culinary arts, with world-class dining and a gourmet cooking school for guests. If you are less interested in preparing your own food than in eating a fine meal, The Greenbrier won't disappoint you. The dining options run the gamut from formal fine dining in the spacious Main Dining Room to a more intimate dinner setting in the Tavern Room to the casual fare at Sam Snead's at the Golf Club. Draper's Café, located on the lower level, is just as chic as the 30 some-odd stores that share the lower level. Regardless of where you choose to dine, the result will be the same — exquisite cuisine artfully presented.

Breakfast Menu

- GRANOLA WITH SPICED PECANS

- MINIATURE PUMPKIN MUFFINS

Dinner Menu

- SMOKED SALMON & SHRIMP TOWER

- MUSHROOM & SPINACH STUFFED CHICKEN BREAST
WITH PERNOD CREAM SAUCE

- SOFT POLENTA
WITH SMITHFIELD HAM

PAN ROASTED ASPARAGUS

GRANNY SMITH SORBET
WITH EDIBLE SPOONS

- *Recipe included*

Golf Pro's Tip

The best thing, in addition to the unique challenges of each of the three courses, is all three start from one clubhouse, with attentive service staff, including experienced caddies, to help savor The Greenbrier experience.

Signature Hole

Greenbrier course, Number 2, par 4 — the tee shot is the most difficult on the course with trees left and a pond to the right. The second shot is all carry to a green guarded by water with bunkers in front and behind. Beautiful hole, but challenging.

Greenbrier Spiced Pecans

*S*weet and spicy, with just a hint of pepper flavor, you'll find lots of uses for these pecans, including the granola recipe that follows. I also used them as the pecans for the Barton Creek Grilled Chicken and Pecan Salad (see page 120). And of course, I ate them out of hand as I sat down to write this chapter.

MAKES 3 CUPS

4 tablespoons (½ stick) butter
¾ cup brown sugar
¾ teaspoon ground cumin
½ teaspoon dry mustard

¼ teaspoon cayenne pepper
1 egg white
3 cups shelled pecan halves

1. Heat the oven to 300°F. Melt the butter in a saucepan over medium-low heat. Stir in the sugar and spices. Stir until sugar mostly dissolves. Remove from heat. Let cool 10 minutes then beat in egg white. Transfer mixture to a large bowl filled with the pecans.

2. Stir to thoroughly coat the pecans. The mixture will be very thick.

3. Spread the pecans on a greased baking sheet in a single layer and bake until pecans are golden brown, about 20 minutes, stirring occasionally.

4. Transfer pecans to another baking sheet to cool. Stir occasionally to prevent clumping. Store in an airtight container for up to 6 weeks, or freeze for up to 3 months.

Greenbrier Granola

Some granolas are so sweet they taste like candy, while others are more like cereal. This crunchy granola is the latter, and a handful tossed on top of a bowl of boring bran flakes tastes like anything but boring bran flakes.

MAKES 6 CUPS

2 tablespoons vegetable oil
⅓ cup honey
⅓ cup pineapple juice
½ teaspoon vanilla extract
¼ teaspoon cinnamon
Pinch of nutmeg
4 cups old-fashioned oats
½ cup coconut

⅓ cup chopped dried apricots
⅓ cup dried tart cherries
⅓ cup dried blueberries
⅓ cup chopped spiced pecans
  (previous recipe)
¼ cup walnuts or
  toasted hazelnuts*

1. Heat the oven to 325°F. Heat first 6 ingredients (oil through nutmeg) in a saucepan over medium-low heat until warm, about 3 to 5 minutes. Do not boil.

2. Mix oats and coconut together in a large mixing bowl. Pour in warm honey syrup and stir to thoroughly coat oats.

3. Spray a large baking sheet with nonstick spray. Spread oat mixture in an even layer on the pan. Bake for 35 to 40 minutes, stirring every 5 to 7 minutes to promote even browning.

4. Remove from oven and mix with dried fruits and nuts. Stir occasionally while cooling to break up lumps. Store at room temperature in an airtight container for up to 1 month, or up to 3 months in the freezer.

To toast hazelnuts, see page 18 under Common Procedures.

Miniature Pumpkin Muffins

These bite-size morsels of warm, spicy pumpkin bread, studded with raisins and pecans have become one of the Greenbrier's most popular breakfast breads. Guests have been known to sneak a few out of the dining room, like puppies hoarding a juicy bone to be devoured later.

MAKES 40 MINI-MUFFINS

8 tablespoons (1 stick) butter, softened
1 cup plus 1 tablespoon sugar, divided
1¼ cups canned pumpkin purée
2 eggs
2 cups flour
2 teaspoons baking powder

2 teaspoons cinnamon, divided
½ teaspoon nutmeg
¼ teaspoon salt
1 cup milk
½ cup chopped pecans
½ cup raisins

1. Heat oven to 375°F. Beat butter and 1 cup of sugar until light and fluffy, about 2 minutes. Stir in the pumpkin. Beat in the eggs, one at a time. If using a mixer (stand or hand), scrape down the sides of the bowl between each addition.

2. Whisk flour, baking powder, 1½ teaspoons cinnamon, nutmeg, and salt together in a bowl.

3. Stir half of flour mixture into pumpkin mixture, then add half the milk. Finish with the remaining flour, then the rest of the milk. Stir just to combine each time. Fold in the nuts and raisins.

4. Spray a miniature muffin pan with nonstick spray. Spoon about 2 tablespoons of batter into each tin, enough to fill three-quarters full (a #50 ice cream scoop works great).

5. Whisk the remaining tablespoon of sugar with the remaining ½ teaspoon of cinnamon. Sprinkle each muffin with a little cinnamon-sugar mixture.

6. Bake until a toothpick inserted in the center comes out clean, about 15 to 18 minutes. Remove from oven, cool a couple of minutes, then remove from pan and cool on a rack.

Smoked Salmon & Shrimp Tower

*L*ayers of smoky salmon pair nicely with cool dill cream cheese. These not only taste divine, they look stunning on a plate, and you can assemble them and the garnishes ahead of time. You need a sharp, 2-inch cookie cutter and 6 molds with a 2-inch diameter and at least 2 inches tall. I used tomato paste cans, both ends removed, washed and dried. (See photograph on page P-18.)

SERVES 6

½ pound sliced smoked salmon
4 large (2 ounces) cooked shrimp, chopped
4 ounces cream cheese, softened
2 tablespoons peeled, seeded and finely chopped tomato
2 teaspoons chopped fresh dill
2 teaspoons chopped fresh chives
1 teaspoon minced red onion

1 teaspoon fresh lemon juice
¼ teaspoon salt
⅛ teaspoon freshly ground black pepper
3 slices multigrain bread

Garnishes (recipes follow):
  Dill cream
  Seasoned cucumber slices
  Chile Lime baby greens

1. Cover a work surface with plastic wrap. Lay smoked salmon on top in a single layer, overlapping slices slightly to create a solid surface with no holes. Cut out 18 circles of salmon with a 2-inch cookie cutter. Reserve salmon scraps. Transfer salmon circles to a small baking sheet and cover with plastic wrap. Refrigerate until needed.

2. Finely chop enough remaining salmon scraps to yield 2 tablespoons. Mix with the chopped shrimp, cream cheese, tomato, dill, chives, red onion, and lemon juice. Season with salt and pepper and mix until thoroughly combined. Chill covered, until needed.

3. Spray the insides of 6 molds (2-inches in diameter and at least 2 inches high) with nonstick spray. Place the molds on a small baking sheet lined with plastic wrap.

4. Pick out the 6 prettiest salmon circles and reserve for the top layer. Place one of the remaining salmon circles in the bottom of a ring mold. Spread 1 tablespoon of the softened cream cheese mixture over the salmon with the back of a spoon until smooth and even. Top with another salmon circle and lightly and evenly press down. Spread another tablespoon of cream cheese mixture over this salmon until smooth and even. Top with a third salmon circle (one of the pretty ones you put aside) and press down. Repeat this process with the remaining 5 ring molds. Refrigerate for at least 1 hour, up to 8 hours.

5. Cut out 6 circles from the multigrain bread with a 2-inch cookie cutter. Toast until lightly golden brown. May be made 1 day in advance, cool, and store in an airtight container at room temperature.

6. Drizzle 6 chilled appetizer plates with a tablespoon each of dill cream.

continued on next page

7. Place a toast piece in the center of a plate. Run a thin knife blade around the inside of a ring mold. Hold the ring mold over the toast circle and gently push the salmon tower out of the mold onto the toast. Repeat with the remaining 5 plates.

8. Overlap seasoned cucumber slices all around the tower and place a mound of baby greens tossed with Chile Lime dressing on one side of the tower.

Dill Cream:
(Makes ½ cup)

½ cup sour cream
Zest of 1 lime
Juice of 1 lime
1 teaspoon finely chopped dill
Dash cayenne pepper
Salt

Whisk all ingredients except salt together in a bowl. Taste and season with salt. Transfer to a clean squeeze bottle, if desired, and chill until needed. May be made 1 day in advance, stored covered in the refrigerator.

Seasoned Cucumber Slices:
(Serves 6)

½ hothouse cucumber
¼ cup rice wine vinegar
¼ teaspoon sugar
Salt and freshly ground black pepper

1. Cut cucumber in half, lengthwise. Cut each half into thin (¼-inch) half-moon slices.

2. Toss with vinegar, sugar, and salt and pepper to taste. May be made a couple of hours in advance.

Chile Lime Baby Greens:

Dressing:
1 teaspoon seeded and minced jalapeño
1 teaspoon lemon zest
Juice of 1 lemon
2 tablespoons soy sauce
1 teaspoon finely chopped parsley
½ teaspoon sugar
½ teaspoon minced garlic
2 tablespoons olive oil
Salt and freshly ground black pepper

5 cups (3 ounces) mixed baby greens

1. Whisk first 7 ingredients (jalapeño through garlic) together. Whisk in olive oil and season with salt and pepper. The mixture will be thicker if made in a blender. May be made 1 day in advance. Store covered in the refrigerator.

2. Toss dressing with baby greens just before serving.

Mushroom & Spinach Stuffed Breast of Chicken

Quite decadent. The Greenbrier stuffs this breast with chicken mousse and lobster meat, and serves it with a licorice-tinged cream sauce. It is quite an involved process, and working with raw meat stuffing can be tricky as it must be kept ice cold and then thoroughly cooked. We had a guest who I knew didn't like lobster, so I tried this without using the raw meat mixtures. I've subsequently written this recipe without the raw meat mixtures, still keeping the integrity of the dish and the key flavors intact. Zac, who rarely eats anything more elaborate than cheeseburgers, agreed to give this simplified version a try. I saw the trepidation in his eyes before he took his first bite, and I watched that fear turn into a smile, then a nod, and finally, a real sense of appreciation. This is why I cook.

SERVES 6

4 teaspoons butter, divided
2 tablespoons minced shallots
2 cups chopped exotic mushrooms
　　(like shiitake, cremini, oyster, etc.)
1 teaspoon minced garlic
¼ cup Madeira
2 tablespoons chopped mixed herbs
　　(tarragon, parsley, etc.)

¼ cup fresh corn kernels, or if frozen,
　　thawed
Salt and freshly ground black pepper
2 cups stemmed fresh spinach leaves,
　　loosely packed
2 tablespoons olive oil, divided
6 (7-ounce) skinned, boned chicken
　　breast halves

To make the stuffing:

1. Heat 3 teaspoons of the butter in a large skillet over medium heat. Add shallots and cook until soft, but not brown, about 1 minute.

2. Stir in the mushrooms and a pinch of salt. Cook until all the moisture has evaporated and the mushrooms are soft, about 5 minutes. Add the garlic and stir. Pour in the Madeira. Cook until wine evaporates, about 2 minutes. Stir in the chopped herbs and corn. Cook until corn is done, stirring frequently, about 2 minutes. Set aside to cool.

3. Melt the remaining 1 teaspoon of butter in a clean pan and cook spinach until wilted, about 3 minutes. Remove from heat and cool completely. When cool, chop spinach and squeeze to remove all liquid.

(Use paper towels or cheesecloth to squeeze out moisture.) Stir spinach into cooled mushroom mixture. Season with salt and pepper. Refrigerate until needed.

To stuff the chicken:

1. Press the thick end of the chicken with the palm of your hand to flatten (give it a couple of good whacks with your hand, or gently use a meat mallet).

2. Place a chicken breast in front of you with the thick end toward you. Insert the tip of a boning knife into the thick end (the knife will be parallel to the cutting board). Gently slide the knife to just below the center of the breast, being careful not to cut through the surface. With small movements, gently work the knife side to side to slightly widen the pocket. The pocket opening should be about 1½

continued on next page

inches long. Don't cut through any other side other than the top opening. Use your finger after you made the knife cut to open up the pocket. Repeat the process with the remaining chicken breasts.

3. Fill each pocket with 2 to 3 tablespoons of stuffing. The breasts will bulge slightly, but not overly. May be made 8 hours in advance up to this point. Cover tightly and refrigerate until ready to cook.

To cook chicken:

1. Heat the oven to 400°F. Season chicken breasts with salt and pepper. Heat 1 tablespoon of olive oil in a large skillet over medium-high heat. Cooking in 2 batches, sear breasts (smooth side down first) until nicely brown. The breasts will release from the pan when ready, about 2 minutes. Don't move them too soon or they will stick. After 2 minutes, give the pan a good shake to loosen the breasts.

2. Turn and brown on the other side, an additional 2 minutes. Repeat searing step with remaining breasts. Transfer breasts, smooth side up, to a baking sheet and finish cooking in the oven until done, about 15 to 18 minutes.

3. Remove from oven, cover loosely with foil, and leave in a warm place for 5 minutes to rest. Then slice each breast on the bias and arrange on a warmed plate. Serve with Pernod Sauce.

Pernod Cream Sauce

*P*ernod is a licorice-flavored liqueur from France. There is just enough of it in this sauce to whisper licorice, but not enough to overpower it. Even non-licorice lovers will appreciate its contribution.

MAKES 1 CUP

8 tablespoons (1 stick) butter, cold
2 tablespoons minced shallots
2 tablespoons white wine
   or dry vermouth

1 cup brown chicken stock*
½ cup heavy cream
2 tablespoons Pernod
Salt and freshly ground black pepper

1. Melt 1 tablespoon butter in a saucepan over medium heat. Add shallots and cook until soft, but not brown, about 1 minute.

2. Pull the pan off the heat and pour in the wine. Return pan to heat and reduce until the liquid almost evaporates, about 1 minute. Turn the heat to medium-high and stir in chicken stock. Bring to a boil, then reduce heat to a strong simmer. Reduce stock by half, about 5 to 8 minutes.

3. Stir in cream and reduce by about ⅓, until it reaches a sauce consistency, about 5 or so minutes. Watch carefully, as cream loves to boil over when you're not watching.

4. Stir in Pernod and remove from heat. Swirl in remaining butter, 1 tablespoon at a time, until all 7 tablespoons have been added and incorporated, returning the pan to low heat if necessary to help melt the butter. Season with salt and pepper. Strain for an ultra smooth sauce.

*Brown chicken stock is richer than regular chicken stock, but the only difference in making the stock is browning the chicken bones before simmering them with the other stock ingredients. If you use a bouillon-based substitute, add ¼ teaspoon of a commercial browning sauce, like Kitchen Bouquet®, to the stock to add color and flavor.

Soft Polenta

WITH SMITHFIELD HAM

Smithfield hams are considered to be the ultimate in country-cured hams. Country-cured hams are significantly more salty than other types of hams. Only those hogs raised in the Smithfield, Virginia area, and processed according to rigorous standards may be called Smithfield hams. The process involves a special dry salt curing, hickory smoking and lengthy aging. I guess you could say this is America's answer to Italy's Prosciutto di Parma, and in fact, prosciutto may be substituted for the Smithfield in this recipe. Smithfield hams may be ordered through the Internet and through some specialty gourmet catalogs. Asiago is an Italian hard cheese made from cow's milk. It has similar grating properties to Parmesan. Serve the polenta as a base for the previous chicken recipe.

SERVES 6

3 tablespoons butter, divided
¼ cup minced onion
3½ to 4 cups chicken stock
1 cup yellow cornmeal
¼ cup grated Asiago
  (or Parmesan) cheese

¼ cup (1 ounce) chopped country
  ham or prosciutto
½ teaspoon salt
¼ teaspoon freshly ground
  black pepper

1. Heat 1 tablespoon of butter in a saucepan over medium heat. Gently cook onions until soft, about 3 to 4 minutes.

2. Pour in 3½ cups of chicken stock and increase heat to medium-high. Slowly whisk in the cornmeal, a little at a time after the stock comes to a boil.

3. Reduce heat to medium and simmer until soft, stirring often, about 10 to 15 minutes. It will pull away from the sides of the pan when done. If it is too thick, thin with chicken stock.

4. Stir 1 tablespoon of butter along with the cheese and ham into the cornmeal. Taste and season with salt and pepper.

5. Pour the polenta into a buttered, heat-resistant bowl or spoon into individual ramekins. Brush surface with remaining tablespoon of butter and cover. Keep hot until ready to serve.

The Northeast

THE SAGAMORE

P.O. Box 450
Bolton Landing, NY 12814
800.358.3585
www.thesagamore.com

Golf Course:
The Sagamore

Designer: Donald Ross

Available holes: 18

Accommodations:
350 guestrooms,
including suites

Rates: $–$$$$

Other Activities:
annual culinary weekend,
Spa, tennis, swimming,
lake activities

Stranded on a private island sounds divine, if that island is in the middle of Lake George in upstate New York and it is home to The Sagamore luxury resort. Of course, a connecting bridge to the mainland removes any chance of real isolation, but one can always dream. Just an hour north of Albany, The Sagamore blends old camp-style Adirondack comfort with perfectly modern amenities. History runs deep at the Sagamore, all the way back to 1883, opening as one of the poshest hotels in the area. A few renovations and more than a century later, the resort continues as one of the swankiest stops for the well-heeled of New York, New England, and beyond.

The Donald Ross-designed golf course sits on 188 acres on the mainland just a short couple of miles away. The picturesque scenery, courtesy of the southern foothills of the Adirondack Mountains, is especially breathtaking during the fall foliage, with captivating shades of golds, reds, and oranges splashed among the stark white birch trunks and giant pines. The English Tudor Clubhouse is homey but elegant, with an outstanding New York-style steakhouse called the Club Grill. Feast on a cocktail of colossal shrimp or traditional oysters Rockefeller while your veal chop sizzles on the grill.

Back on the island, dining is a bit more formal, especially in the award-winning Trillium fine dining venue, featuring global cuisine, and well worth the effort to dress for dinner. Mr. Brown's Pub (named after the founder of The Sagamore) is rustically decorated in Adirondack style, and serves American eclectic cuisine, like salmon, ribs, and chicken. The resort offers other dining options on a seasonal basis, like afternoon tea and evening cocktails on the Veranda.

Breakfast Menu

- OATMEAL BRÛLÉE

- SMOKED SALMON MONTE CRISTO

Dinner Menu

APPLE-DUSTED SALMON WITH JÍCAMA SLAW

- PAN-SEARED LAMB CHOPS
WITH ROSEMARY PESTO & NATURAL JUS

- RATATOUILLE

MINTED PEARL COUSCOUS

- CHOCOLATE CROISSANT BREAD PUDDING

- *Recipe included*

Golf Pro's Tip

As Donald Ross courses dictate, it is better to sacrifice a little distance to keep the ball in play.

Signature Hole

Number 13, par 4 — with blind water to the right and thick pine trees to the left, a straight tee shot is crucial. Move up an extra club on the second shot, as more water lies to the left near the uphill green.

Sagamore Oatmeal Brûlée

Don't like oatmeal that much? Betcha you'll like it better it this way. My husband thought it was dessert, and almost turned it down at 7:00 in the morning. Now he's glad he didn't. The crisp burnt sugar topping adds a pleasantly bitter sweetness while the nuts and raisins add texture to otherwise boring oats. This dish inspired our gym-buddy, Dick, to experiment with other fruit and nut combinations, like peaches and pecans. Use your imagination and try your own combination. (See photograph on page P-19.)

SERVES 6

5¾ cups water
¾ teaspoon salt
3 cups old-fashioned oats
¼ cup raisins
¼ cup toasted walnuts*

¼ cup applesauce
¼ cup maple syrup
12 tablespoons brown sugar
Fresh berries and mint

1. Heat broiler to high (see note). Bring the water and salt to a strong boil. Stir in oats. Reduce heat and cook 7 minutes, stirring occasionally. Remove from heat and cover. Let rest 5 minutes, or until all of the water has been absorbed and oatmeal is thick and creamy.

2. Fold in the raisins, walnuts, applesauce, and maple syrup.

3. Divide the oatmeal mixture evenly among 6 (8-ounce) ovenproof custard cups. Sprinkle 2 tablespoons of brown sugar evenly on top of each cup.

4. Place custard cups on a baking sheet and place under broiler (about 3 inches from heat) and brown tops, about 1 to 3 minutes depending upon the heat of your broiler. Watch carefully! Remove from heat and cool a couple of minutes. Using oven mitts, place hot cups onto serving plates.

5. Garnish with fresh berries and mint.

NOTE: Alternatively, use a kitchen torch to brown the tops. The advantage of a kitchen torch is that it doesn't heat the custard cups as much, but the disadvantage is that it takes longer to caramelize than the broiler.

*To toast nuts, see page 18 under Common Procedures.

Smoked Salmon Monte Cristo

*A*n elegant brunch entrée, the real benefit is in the taste. Smoked salmon and Brie are exquisite together, and the arugula adds a peppery bite. The resort serves this with a truffle-laced hollandaise sauce, but I found that it was rich enough without the hollandaise. I also substituted sourdough bread for the potato dill bread that the resort makes from scratch for this recipe.

SERVES 2

¼ cup cream cheese, softened
1 tablespoon fresh chopped dill
  (more for garnish)
4 slices sourdough or potato
  dill bread
3 ounces smoked salmon

6 ounces Brie cheese, rind removed
  and cut into 12 equal chunks
1 cup arugula
3 eggs
1 cup milk
1 tablespoon butter

1. Mix the cream cheese and dill together until smooth. Spread a thin layer of this mixture on one side of each bread slice.

2. Top 2 of the bread slices with equal amounts of the salmon, covering the surface. Dot the Brie chunks evenly over the salmon and cover the cheese with the arugula. Top with the remaining 2 pieces of bread.

3. Trim the sandwiches to a square shape, discarding the crusts. (This much can be done the night before. Wrap each sandwich tightly in plastic wrap and then store in another airtight container. Unwrap sandwiches before proceeding with step 4 the next morning.)

4. Beat the eggs with the milk for an egg dip.

5. Melt the butter in a nonstick skillet over medium heat.

6. Dip the sandwiches in the egg dip and fry until golden brown on both sides, about 2 to 3 minutes per side.

7. Cut the sandwiches into 3 equal rectangles each, or cut in half on the diagonal for a different shape. Garnish with fresh dill.

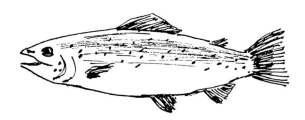

Pan-Seared Lamb Chops

WITH ROSEMARY PESTO

*T*he high heat from the oven combined with the oil from the pesto translates into a bit of a smoky kitchen, but once you taste the garlicky herb crust, you won't mind a little smoke. Just open your windows and pour your guests another glass of wine.

SERVES 6

3 (8-bone) lamb racks, about
   3 pounds

Rosemary Pesto:
4 tablespoons toasted pine nuts*
2 tablespoons roughly chopped garlic
1 cup (1 ounce) loosely packed fresh
   rosemary leaves

2 cups (1 ounce) loosely packed fresh
   basil leaves
⅔ cup olive oil
4 tablespoons grated Asiago or
   Parmesan cheese
Salt and freshly ground black pepper
Natural Jus (recipe follows)

1. Pulse the pine nuts, garlic, and herbs in a food processor until mixture is paste-like. Slowly drizzle in olive oil with the machine running. Stir in the cheese and season with salt and pepper.

2. Cut each lamb rack into 4 pieces (2 bones per piece). Brush lamb generously with pesto and marinate 1 hour at room temperature or up to 8 hours in the refrigerator.

3. Heat the oven to 400°F. Heat an ovenproof skillet over high heat until extremely hot. Sear the lamb chops on all sides (about 5 minutes in total) and place in the oven to finish cooking. You don't need to add extra oil to the pan to sear, as the marinade has plenty of oil.

4. Cook the chops to rare (120°F), about 4 minutes or medium-rare (130°F), about 8

minutes. Remove from oven, place on a baking sheet (with sides) and cover with foil. Let rest 5 minutes before serving. Meanwhile make jus in the same pan in which you roasted the lamb. Use an oven mitt to cover the extremely hot handle.

Natural Jus:
½ cup red wine
1 cup lamb or beef stock
Salt and freshly ground black pepper

1. Heat pan with lamb drippings over medium-high heat. Add ½ cup red wine and boil until only 2 tablespoons remain, scraping the bottom of the pan to loosen any browned bits.

2. Add 1 cup of lamb or beef stock and simmer 5 minutes. Season with salt and pepper.

Ratatouille

Ratatouille dishes are great because they can be served warm or at room temperature, and taste even better the next day. This one has a refreshing tomato taste and a nice crunch from the vegetables. Surprisingly, it doesn't have onions, so if you are from Provence, feel free to toss in some chopped or sliced onions when you add the eggplant. I'm one of those proponents of salting eggplant before cooking it to remove its bitterness. Some chefs say it doesn't matter. There is no right or wrong answer; it's just a matter of personal taste.

SERVES 6

1 small eggplant (about 1 pound)
1 teaspoon salt
1 small zucchini (about 7 ounces)
1 small summer squash
   (about 7 ounces)
2 tablespoons olive oil
2 tablespoons minced garlic
1 red bell pepper, seeded
   and chopped

1 tomato (about 8 ounces) seeded
   and chopped
2 tablespoons chopped fresh oregano
2 tablespoons chopped fresh basil
½ cup tomato juice
Salt and freshly ground
   black pepper

1. Cut the eggplant into ½-inch slices and sprinkle with 1 teaspoon of salt. Set aside for 30 minutes. Rinse and pat dry with paper towels. Cut slices into ½-inch cubes.

2. Cut zucchini and summer squash into ½-inch cubes.

3. Heat the oil in a wide saucepan over medium heat. Stir in the eggplant and garlic. Cook for 2 minutes, stirring

frequently. Add the zucchini and summer squash, cooking another 2 minutes, stirring frequently, until vegetables begin to soften.

4. Stir in the red bell pepper, tomatoes, and herbs, simmering until the vegetables are soft, about 2 minutes. Stir in the tomato juice and cook until heated through. Season with salt and pepper.

B. Hillis

Chocolate Croissant Bread Pudding

*T*here is always one dessert in each of my books that I go ga-ga over. It was the Molten Mexican Chocolate Ecstasy in *The Great Ranch Cookbook,* and the Chocolate Volcano in *The Cool Mountain Cookbook.* This recipe is this book's killer dessert. (Are you seeing a chocolate pattern here?) My neighbor Marilyn threatened to cut off my egg borrowing privileges if I didn't give her the recipe immediately. She's now made it more than I have, and that's a lot. It's incredible right out of the oven and equally wonderful cold, the next day. Start this recipe the night before you plan to serve it.

SERVES 8

2½ ounces semisweet chocolate, chopped
1 ounce unsweetened chocolate, chopped
½ vanilla bean, split
2 cups heavy cream

¾ cup sugar
3 whole eggs
2 egg yolks
1 teaspoon butter
10 ounces day-old croissants, torn into pieces

1. Melt both chocolates slowly in the top of a double boiler set over simmering water.

2. Meanwhile, scrape the seeds out of the vanilla bean into a saucepan with the cream and sugar. (Save vanilla bean to flavor sugar or discard.) Bring mixture to a boil over medium heat, stirring occasionally. As soon as the mixture boils, remove from heat.

3. Whisk the melted chocolate into the hot cream mixture until smooth.

4. Beat the eggs and yolks together in a bowl. Place a damp towel underneath the bowl to anchor it. Slowly drizzle about half of the hot chocolate mixture into the eggs, a little at a time, whisking constantly. If you add too much too soon, you'll curdle the eggs.

5. After the eggs are warm to the touch, whisk into the remaining chocolate cream. Set the bowl in a larger bowl of ice water, stirring frequently to cool to room temperature, about 10 minutes.

6. Butter an 8 x 8-inch baking pan and toss in the torn croissants. The pan will be full. Slowly pour the cooled chocolate mixture into the pan, pouring all over the exposed bread. The bread won't be completely submerged, but make sure it has all been moistened with the chocolate custard. Cover and chill overnight, or for at least 4 hours.

7. Remove the baking pan from the refrigerator and heat the oven to 325°F. Set the pudding pan inside of a large roasting pan in the oven. Add very hot water to the roasting pan to come half way up the sides of the pudding pan.

8. Bake, uncovered, until a knife inserted in the center of the pudding comes out clean, about 1 hour to 1 hour and 10 minutes. Cool 15 minutes and cut into squares to serve. If there is any left, store covered in the refrigerator, up to 3 days.

Sources

■ Anything and everything:

A. J.'s Fine Foods
23251 N. Pima Rd.
Scottsdale, AZ 85255
480.563.5070

7141 E. Lincoln Dr.
Scottsdale, AZ 85253
480.998.0052

5017 N. Central Ave.
Phoenix, AZ 85012
602.230.7015

13226 N. 7th St.
Phoenix, AZ 85022
602.230.7015

7131 W. Ray Road #37
Chandler, AZ 85226
480.705.0011

A. J.'s is still my favorite grocery store. If I can't find something in a regular grocery store, I can count on A. J.'s to either have it on hand, or find it for me. Their customer service continues to exceed my expectations, especially at the Pima location in North Scottsdale. Give them a call, and tell them I sent you, or visit their website at *www.ajsfinefoods.com*.

■ Blue Cheese:

Maytag Dairy Farms
P.O. Box 806
Newton, IA 50208
800.247.2458

America's most famous blue cheese was first produced in 1941. It's my favorite blue cheese, more creamy than European cheeses, like Roquefort and Gorgonzola. The smallest amount you can order is 2 pounds. Find a neighbor who'd like to split it with you.

■ Ceylon Cinnamon:

Penzeys Spices
P.O. Box 933
Muskego, WI 53150
800.741.7787
www.penzeys.com

Penzeys is the premier spice company. I found Ceylon cinnamon in one of their stores in Minnesota and tried it. They had a row of all their cinnamon types, so I was able to taste and compare them. This was my favorite. It's so delicate, almost floral, and much better than the harsh cinnamon we get in the grocery stores. Of course, sometimes a strong cinnamon is needed, especially in quick breads and cakes that contain multiple sweet spices.

■ Chef Tools:

Kitchen Classics
4041 E. Thomas Rd.
Phoenix, AZ 85018
602.954.8141
www.kitchenclassics.com

KC is my favorite independent cooking store in Phoenix. The selection is wide, and the service is the best. Check out their site and sign up for a weekly recipe.

Sur La Table
www.surlatable.com

The Internet shop is almost as much fun as their brick and mortar shops-almost. Good selection of mini-tart pans, dessert molds, and ice-cream scoops. If they don't have what you're looking for, ask them, they might be able to order it for you. If you're ever in Seattle, you must visit the original shop across from Pike Place Market.

■ Coffee and Espresso:

Cave Creek Coffee Company
P.O. Box 4390
Cave Creek, AZ 85327
480.488.0603
www.cavecreekcoffee.com

Cowboy Beans and Cowgirl Beans are favorites in this unique java shop. Dave's added a wine-tasting bar, so if you're in Cave Creek, AZ, stop by and say hello.

Little City Roasting Company
Three Austin, TX locations:
www.littycity.com

2604 Guadalupe
Austin, TX 78705
512.467.2326

916 Congress
Austin, TX 78701
512.476.2489

603 N. Lamar
Austin, TX 78703
(inside Bookpeople bookstore)
512.472.5050

Fresh-roasted coffee blends, including some killer custom blends. Owner Donna Taylor-DiFrank has kept Austin buzzing since 1993. Little City gladly ships.

■ Gourmet Foods & Housewares:

Paul's Pantry at El Pedregal
P.O. Box 2207
Carefree, AZ 85377
480.488.4300
www.paulspantry.com

This independent gourmet foods and tabletop shop is delightful. The specialty foods, dishes, and accessories are unique, many with a decidedly Southwest flavor, like prickly pear syrup. Of course, you'll also find other specialties, including white truffle oil. All the food shots we took were styled using housewares from Paul's Pantry. Visit them on the Internet and ask to be put on their mailing list.

■ Smithfield Hams:

The Smithfield Collection
P.O. Box 250, Portsmouth, VA 23705
800.628.2242
www.smithfieldcollection.com

Although there are many brands of salty country hams, Smithfield hams are known as the premier southern country ham.

■ Sauces:

Custom Food Products, Inc.
800.553.9896
www.customfoods.com

Custom Food Products makes the best demi-glace I've ever tasted that wasn't made from scratch, and frankly, it's better than some restaurant-made demi-glaces. The brand is Custom Master's Touch Sauce Bases Demi-Glace. The bad news is they don't sell directly to consumers. A. J.'s Fine Foods (the Pima location) stocks this and the hollandaise sauce. I provided the contact information so that you can ask your specialty grocer to order it for you. An 11-ounce jar retails for about $11.00, and will make 16 or so cups of demi-glace, using 3 tablespoons of demi to 1 cup of boiling water.

More Than Gourmet
929 Home Avenue
Akron, OH 44310
800.860.9385
www.morethangourmet.com

In addition to demi-glace and several chicken stock options, More Than Gourmet also offers some unusual sauce bases, including venison, duck, and seafood. More Than Gourmet has good distribution in specialty grocery stores, or you can visit them on the Internet.

■ Southwestern Ingredients & Pepper Grill:

Jane Butel's Pecos Valley Spice Company
P.O. Box 964
Albuquerque, NM 87103
800.473.8226
www.pecosvalley.com

Extensive collection of southwestern ingredients, including blue cornmeal, Mexican oregano, cumin, dried chile pods (like ancho) and fresh ground pure chile. Noted southwestern author and cooking teacher, Jane Butel, is the star behind this specialty company. Check out her 16 cookbooks and her cooking school, too.

Santa Fe School of Cooking
116 W. San Francisco Street
Santa Fe, NM 87501
800.982.4688
www.santafeschoolofcooking.com

The Internet catalog has a plethora of southwestern dried chiles (whole and ground) and spices. They also sell a pepper grill that fits over you gas burner and allows you to fire-roast several peppers at once. If you're in Santa Fe, you should stop by their store off the square, and maybe even catch a class in their southwestern kitchen.

Acknowledgements

I'm so very blessed to have so many people contribute to the success of this book. From the generous staff at each of the resorts, to the talented publishing professionals who lent their expertise, to hungry friends and neighbors, and finally, to my incredibly supportive family, this book is a compilation of all our efforts. I hope you enjoy reading and cooking from this book as much as I delighted in putting it together. See you in the kitchen.

To Jeff, my husband, for his unwavering love and support. The beautiful food photography in this book is the result of his talent behind the camera.

To Olin Ashley, my father and editor. He still has a knack for rearranging my words without changing my voice. I'm so grateful for his love and guidance.

To Jerry Ashley, my mother. She is still my best friend and biggest fan.
Her encouragement keeps me going and she never lets me give up.

To Betsy Hillis, my illustrator. Her talent with pen and paper continues to astonish me.

To Christy Moeller-Masel and Kelly Scott at ATG Productions, Avondale, AZ.
Award-winning cover designs are their specialty, and I'm fortunate to have them on my team.
It was their idea to create the huge golf ball on the front cover.
I know their work on *The Cool Mountain Cookbook* helped us garner
a finalist position in the national Benjamin Franklin Awards.

To Michele DeFilippo at 1106 Design, Phoenix. Her work on *The Cool Mountain Cookbook* won an award for Best Interior Design by the Arizona Book Publishing Association, so it was only natural that I work with her again on this book.

To Tom Hummel at Toppan Printing. Once again, Tom came to my rescue and helped me navigate the complex world of printing. His calmness is always the perfect balance to my intensity, and he makes me laugh.

To the entire staff at Paul's Pantry gourmet shop —
Paul, Lorna, Erma, Rita, Nancy, Kathleen, and Cindy. All of the food shots we took look as good as they do because we used the tableware from Paul's Pantry. The staff never complained once during my weekend raids of their shelves for our shoots.

To Gaye Ingram, CCP, author of *Webster's New World Dictionary of Culinary Arts*. Her book is the most important book in my culinary library. I used it everyday during the writing phase of this book. The best part, though, is that she is my friend, and I could pick up the phone and call her when I needed her opinion. Get her book if you don't have it. It's a godsend. I also want to thank Gaye for proofreading the manuscript when she had better things to do. Her insightful comments have made this a much better book.

To Susan Prieskorn and Letty Flatt, multi-talented pastry chefs. Letty's husband, Robbie, calls her work conversations "muffin-talk." I needed lots of muffin-talk with these two experts when it came time to bake, and each generously shared her knowledge. Letty's book, *Chocolate Snowball*, is available through her website at ***www.chocolatesnowball.com.***

To Chef Cathy Rosenburg. Her attention to detail was a lifesaver for me as she poured over every word of the text, checking for clarity, accuracy, and making sure I didn't butcher the French terms.

To Michael McLaughlin, prolific cookbook author and food writer. My love affair with cooking was heavily influenced by Michael's 1993 book, *Cooking for the Weekend.* I've since tried to buy every book he's written because his recipes are creative, innovative, and clearly presented. Michael's voice is conversational, like you're talking with a dear friend. I try to write my books in a similar fashion.

To Antonio Allegra, author, editor, and writing coach. Toni is a warm, generous, caring mentor. She's offered gentle encouragement and advice to me throughout my culinary career. I respect her opinion and value her friendship.

To Robin Kline, food writer and consultant. Positive thinking oozes from Robin, like a bubbling brook. She's an encouraging mentor and cherished friend.

To Sherrie Buzby, photographer. Sherrie gave up a Saturday to come and teach us a few tips about food photography, and all she wanted in return was a home-cooked meal.

To John Brinkmann, Foothills Photo, Carefree, AZ. John convinced us to experiment with different slide film for the photos, and was generous with his time and knowledge.

To Marilyn Robertson, neighbor and friend. Marilyn was always available to retest a recipe, take a dish off my hands so it wouldn't go to waste, or provide me with an ingredient I was sure I had but didn't. She was invariably there just when I needed her.

To Rosalie and Alex Passovoy, neighbors and friends. Rosalie and Alex would come at the blink of an eye to help me taste and critique the recipes. They also let me borrow their granddaughter Emmy and daughter-in-law Nancy, on one occasion to help taste.

To Pat and Jan Johnston, next door neighbors and friends. They took samples at all times of the day and night, helping me evaluate which recipes to include, and the feedback was always detailed and helpful.

To Pete & Malen Eyerly, neighbors and friends. I didn't get as many dishes as planned over to their house, as they were avoiding my calories like the plague. I did get their opinions on the spa dishes, and that was helpful, as other neighbors weren't as willing to try those recipes. Imagine that.

To Donna Bachman, friend and former chef. Donna helped with encouraging words, tasting recipes, and sharing wine. What else could a girl ask for?

To all my other tasters, willing or not. Shirley and Erv Daskow, Kathy and Al Keir, Mark and Andrea Korff, Susan and Steve Lefkowitz, Candy and Quentin Van Camp, Dee and Billy Moore, Lou Robertson, Lisa Mackey, Denise Bina, Gary Wolf, Lisa Amore, Chris Meleshko, Joe Ferry, Tom Flemming, and Bill Twitty.

And last, but certainly not least, I graciously want to thank
the incredibly helpful staff at each resort:

The Lodge at Pebble Beach:
Valerie Ramsey, Jeff Jake, and Chuck Dunbar.

The Broadmoor:
Allison Scott, Craig Reed, and Russ Miller.

The Lodge at Koele:
Andrew Manion-Copley, Brendan Moynahan , Babs Harrison, and Michele Lee.

Manele Bay Hotel:
Edwin Goto, Doug Stephenson, Babs Harrison, and Michele Lee.

Bandon Dunes:
Paul Moss, Marla Taylor, Tim Hval, and Ian Sperling.

The Boulders:
Rita Ferraro, Mary Nearn, and Tom McCahan.

The Fairmont Scottsdale Princess:
Sue Kavanagh, Lita de Iongh, Reed Groban, Mark McCleary, and Bill Grove.

The Lodge at Ventana Canyon:
Carla Whitney, Alan Sanchez, and Dave Schneider.

Loews Ventana Canyon:
Kimberly Sundt and Jim Makinson.

The Phoenician:
Marguarite Clark, James Boyce, and John Jackson.

Barton Creek:
Martha Heagany, Jenny Holland, Chip Gist, and Kevin Newbolt.

Coconut Point:
Kim Cisewski, Thomas Martin, Jay Garrick, and Kerri Meehan.

Doral Golf & Spa:
Angela Berardino, Jodi Cross, Jackeline Abreu, and Michael Miraglia.

Grand Cypress:
Kathy Cattoor, Kenneth Juran, Bill Rowden, and Kris Michalson.

The Cloisters:
Judi Griggs, Kara Norman, Todd Rogers, and Brannen Veal.

Pinehurst:
Stephen Boyd, Paul Ramsey, and Lew Ferguson.

The Homestead:
Niki Gribbin, Albert Schnarwyler, and Don Ryder.

The Greenbrier:
Lynn Swann, Riki Senn, Robert Harris, and Laura Gustafson.

The Sagamore:
Trisha Hayes, Thomas Guay, and Tom Smack.

Index

Par Fork!
The Golf Resort Cookbook

P.O. Box 5165 · Carefree, AZ 85377 · 480.595.0890 (fax)
www.penandfork.com

Please send:

_____Copies of *Par Fork! The Golf Resort Cookbook*
@ $23.95 each ....$ _____

_____Copies of *The Cool Mountain Cookbook:*
A Gourmet Guide to Winter Retreats @ $19.95 each ....$ _____

_____Copies of *The Great Ranch Cookbook:*
Spirited Rhetoric and Recipes from America's Best
Guest Ranches @ $19.95 each..$ _____

Shipping:

$4.00 for 1st book...$ _____

$2.00 for each additional book...$ _____

Subtotal...$ _____

AZ residents add 8.1% tax ....$ _____

Total..$ _____

Enclose a check made payable to Pen and Fork

Shipping information *(please print):*

Name _____

Address _____

City, State, Zip_____

Phone _____

Email_____

Would you like to be added to our monthly email newsletter? ❏ Yes   ❏ No

Would you like the book(s) autographed? If yes, to whom? *(please print)*

_____